28

$12.00

The DESTROYER

THE DESTROYER

The Antichrist Is At Hand

TEXE MARRS

RCP RiverCrest Publishing
1708 Patterson Road • Austin, Texas 78733

ACKNOWLEDGEMENTS

My staff deserves maximum praise for their outstanding contributions. Included: Michelle Powell, business administrator, Sandra Myers, publishing and art; Jerry Barrett, computer and internet; Nelson Sorto, shipping and facilities manager; and Steve Reilly, administration and shipping. To my wife and confidant, Wanda Marrs, goes all my love and gratefulness.

The Destroyer

Cover design: Texe Marrs and Sandra Myers

Cover graphic Copyright: Jesse-lee Lang / 123RF Stock Photo

Printed in the United States of America

Library of Congress Catalog Card Number 20166946469

Categories: 1. Religion 2. Bible Prophecy 3. Christianity 4. Judaism

ISBN 978-1-930004-00-9

He Is Antichrist

Who is a liar but he that denieth that Jesus is the Christ? He is antichrist, that denieth the Father and the Son.

Whosoever denieth the Son, the same hath not the Father: but he that acknowledgeth the Son hath the Father also.

—I John 2:22-23

Other Books by RiverCrest Publishing

Holy Serpent of the Jews, by Texe Marrs

Pastors and Churches Gone Wild, by Texe Marrs

DNA Science and the Jewish Bloodline, by Texe Marrs

Conspiracy of the Six-Pointed Star, by Texe Marrs

Conspiracy World, by Texe Marrs

Mysterious Monuments: Encyclopedia of Secret Illuminati Designs, Masonic Architecture, and Occult Places, by Texe Marrs

Codex Magica: Secret Signs, Mysterious Symbols and Hidden Codes of the Illuminati, by Texe Marrs

Matrix of Gog: From the Land of Magog Came the Khazars to Destroy and Plunder, by Daniel Patrick

Synagogue of Satan: The Secret History of Jewish World Domination, by Andrew Carrington Hitchcock

Protocols of the Learned Elders of Zion

Days of Hunger, Days of Chaos, by Texe Marrs

Project L.U.C.I.D.: The Beast 666 Universal Human Control System, by Texe Marrs

Circle of Intrigue: The Hidden Inner Circle of the Global Illuminati Conspiracy, by Texe Marrs

Dark Majesty: The Secret Brotherhood and the Magic of a Thousand Points of Light, by Texe Marrs

New Age Cults and Religions, by Texe Marrs

Mystery Mark of the New Age, by Texe Marrs

Dark Secrets of the New Age, by Texe Marrs

For additional information we highly recommend the following website:

www.powerofprophecy.com

TABLE OF Contents

PART I

The Son of Perdition

ONE

The Destroyer: "He That Hath Ears to Hear, Let Him Hear"

"Let no man deceive you by any means: for that day shall not come, except there come a falling away first, and that man of sin be revealed, the son of perdition.... Even him, whose coming is after the working of Satan with all power and signs and lying wonders."

—II Thessalonians 2:3,9

"He that hath ears to hear, let him hear."

—Jesus Christ
Matthew 11:15

Evening beckons. Dark thunderclouds gather. "Night cometh," warned our Lord Jesus, "when no man can work."

At Jesus coming in the flesh, the people of Israel were not

ready to accept him. As Christ began His ministry, He noted the apathetic silence of the Israel nation. It was, he said, as if the children had piped music to the people in the crowded market, but still, lamentably, no one heard. The people went about their business like deaf mutes, oblivious to the opportunity that visited them.

"He that hath ears to hear," said Christ, "let him hear" *(Matthew 11:15)*.

Israel heard not and so they killed the King of Glory on the cross.

Now, almost 2,000 years later, I write this book, a book that reveals the coming of another "Christ," a man wholly different than Jesus. A man whom the Bible calls, *"The Destroyer."*

Who, I lamentably ask, who has ears to hear?

Death, Evil, Pestilence

The Bible has much to say about the Destroyer. In *Exodus 12:23,* he is the death agent who kills the first-born in Egypt. In *Job 33:22* the Destroyer (literally "they which cause to die") are angels of death that are ready to take a man's life during severe illness. In *2 Samuel 24:16-17*, the Destroyer is the angel that destroys the people by pestilence, and in *Psalms 78:49*, the Destroyer signals the "evil angels."

We find, however, the Destroyer at his horrible worst in the book of *Revelation. Revelation* speaks of the star who falls from heaven unto the earth. To him was given the key of the bottomless pit. Unlocked, there arose out of the pit the smoke of a great furnace. And there came out of the smoke supernatural, locust-like creatures empowered for a time to plague and torment the men and women of earth who have not God.

"And in those days shall men seek death, and shall

> *not find it; and shall desire to die, and death shall flee from them."*
>
> *—Revelation 9:6*

They Have a King Over Them

The Scriptures reveal to us that these monstrous creatures have a king over them:

> *"And they had a king over them, which is the angel of the bottomless pit, whose name in the Hebrew tongue is Abaddon, but in the Greek tongue hath his name Apollyon."*
>
> *—Revelation 9:11*

Note the name of the king that is the dark angel of the bottomless pit. His name in the Hebrew language is *Abaddon.* The Hebrew dictionary tells us the meaning of the word Abaddon is the *Destroyer*.

We discover also, in *Revelation 11:7* that the king, or dark angel, of the bottomless pit is the beast. *The beast, therefore, is the Destroyer.*

In Freemasonry, the phallic cult whose rituals are based on the Jewish Kabbalah, the Mason discovers in a higher degree that the *"Sacred Name"* is *Abaddon.* This is evidence that Freemasonry, like its parent, the religion of Judaism, is in allegiance to the beast, and to the dragon (Satan).

It is the dragon (Satan or Lucifer), say the Scriptures, who gives the beast (the Destroyer) "his power, and his seat, and great authority" *(Revelation 13:2)*.

> *"And they (the unredeemed people of earth) worshipped the dragon which gave power unto the beast: and they worshipped the beast, saying, Who*

is like unto the beast? Who is able to make war with him?" —*Revelation 13:4*

The Destroyer is none other than the beast, who opens his mouth in blasphemy against God and who makes war against the saints. Power is given him over all peoples and nations.

"And all that dwell upon the earth shall worship him, whose names are not written in the book of life of the Lamb slain from the foundation of the world."
—*Revelation 13:8*

"If Any Man Have an Ear, Let Him Hear"

And the very next verse *(Revelation 13:9)* states: *"If any man have an ear, let him hear."* This was the same proclamation preached when Jesus came and his ministry began (*Matthew 11:15*).

Now, it is proclaimed once again to signal the coming of the wicked and malicious Antichrist, the beast whom we know as the Destroyer. Once more we see that all but the redeemed who know and serve Jesus shall be taken by surprise when the Destroyer emerges from the bottomless pit to bring havoc and death to the world and take peace from mankind and replace it with the terrors of war.

The Destroyer, whom all the world worships, and who requires all humanity to take either the number, or the name, or the mark of the beast, will put to death every one who refuses. Their death will be by beheading.

55 Bible Proofs About Antichrist Presented In This Book

Through study of the prophetic Scriptures, we can know the people, or nation, from which the Destroyer, the antichrist, will spring. In the latter part of this book, I present to you 55 biblical proofs that it is the Jews, the nation that is called by the rabbis themselves, the *"People of the Serpent."*

Jesus stood up to the blind and belligerent leaders of the Jews in the midst of their challenging and blaspheming of Him. He angrily responded: *"Ye Serpents, ye generation of vipers, how can ye escape the damnation of hell?" (Matthew 23:33).*

It is, then, a certitude that the Jews are serpents, and are history's great destroyers. And today they perform their destructive activities and abominations under the watchful eye of the Destroyer, who guides them and soon will emerge to lead them direct to their hellish destiny.

History of the Destroyers

History records a long chronology of the Jews as destroyers. Eustace Mullins, noted author, in his *The New History of the Jews*, states, "The fact is that the Jews were known only as destroyers in the ancient world." Mullins statement is backed up by Rome's Tacitus, by Israel's own historian extraordinarre, Josephus, and by Gibbons in his famous *History of the Decline and Fall of the Roman Empire*.

Modern history also reveals that the Jews continue to be destroyers; Moreover, the more perceptive of the Jews recognize this trait amongst their own tribe and are proud of it. Destruction, they say, is what the *Babylonian Talmud*, their most holy book, requires of them as Jews. The Jews destroy the present world, they explain, in order to achieve their idealized future world as Conquerors and Gods.

Maurice Samuel, celebrated Jewish author of two pro-Zionist books in the 1920s, *You Gentiles* (1924) and *I, The Jew* (1927), well understood the kabbalist doctrine that this present-day world must be destroyed to make way for the inauguration of the serpentine future world. Samuel, like other kabbalists, believed that the Gentile world must come to a revolutionary end, and he saw the communist Jews and their Red Terror as a prelude and means toward to that end. In *You Gentiles*, Samuel wrote:

> "We Jews. We are the destroyers and will remain the destroyers. Nothing you do will meet our demands and needs. We will forever destroy, because we want a world of our own, a God-World, which it is not in your nature to build."

Samuel wrote many books later in the 40s, 50s, and 60s which confirmed his kabbalistic, devil views, including *The Great Hatred* (1940), *The Web of Lucifer* (1947), and *The Second Crucifixion* (1960). His name is found in *Who's Who in World Jewry* (1972 edition).

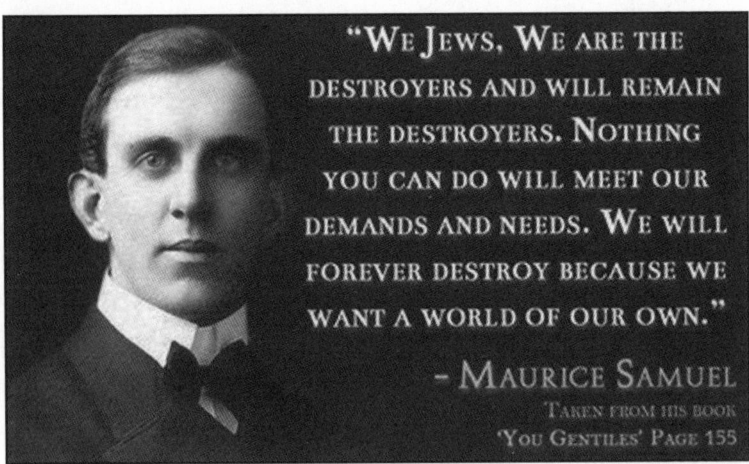

The Russian Revolution of 1917 and the subsequent Red Terror perpetrated by the monstrous regime of the communist Jews seems to have excited and thrilled Jews all over the world. In the United States, Rabbi Stephen Wise, a friend and contemporary of President Franklin D. Roosevelt, boasted of the "great achievement" of Jews Lenin and Trotsky, and he gushed at the "insightful works" of Karl Marx. "Communism is Judaism," Wise exulted, "and Judaism is Communism."

Now, as we reach the end of the second decade of the third millennium, the Jews are still prideful of the manner in which their Jewish counterparts a century ago manipulated the gigantic nation of Russia and engineered the advancement of communism by the Jews. They knew that this war was simply a dress rehearsal for the coming *Day of Purification* when their lord and god, Leviathan the Holy Serpent, shall rise from the abyss to put an end to the rule of the Goyim (Gentiles).

Even as I write this book, I realize that the Jews' devilish sabbatian religion, toxin-producing culture, and insidious hatred of other races and nationalities drives the People of the Serpent on toward their foul and deceitful goal of global domination. Today, the Jewish elite are using the colossal destabilization of country after country in the Middle East—carried out by the U.S.A. and other allies—and the consequent migration of millions of displaced Moslems to further their ends. As Angela Davis, the black radical and revolutionary recently stated, "Communism has morphed into new systems, but has the very same goals. Asylum is the catchword for today and migration and resettlement is the movement of the 21st century."

As Oscar Levy, noted Jewish scholar, remarked in his preface to the book, *World Significance of the Russian Revolution* (1920):

> "There is scarcely an event in modern Europe that cannot be traced back to the Jew. We Jews are today nothing else but the world's seducers, its *destroyers*, its incendiaries, its executioners."

Famous illustration by Gustave Doré, *Destruction of Leviathan* (1865). The Jewish Kabbalah and Talmud teach that Leviathan (*Job 41*) is a good angel and a constant helpmate and guide for Jews. It is further taught that Leviathan will be the messiah who elevates the Jews to victory and world domination in the future to come. Obviously, this is drastically different from Christianity which warns that the dragon and serpent is the Devil, or Satan, an evil rebel against God and His saints.

Today, the destroyers are actively working to usher in the age of blood and demonic endeavor. They are at the forefront of every wicked movement, from same sex marriage and transgenderism to the engineering of the climate and technological transhumanism. Their methods may change but, as Angela Davis noted, their dark goals remain exactly the same.

The Parable of the Vineyard and the Husbandmen

Jesus our Lord gave us a wise parable that illuminates these goals of the Jews. He told the chief priests and elders of the Jews the story of the husbandmen who were lessees (renters) of a vineyard, which had a winepress and a tower. The absentee owner of the vineyard and its lands, from a far land where he resided, sent his servants to the husbandmen, that they might receive the first fruits of the harvest.

> *"And the husbandmen took his servants, and beat one, and killed another, and stoned another. Again, he sent other servants more than the first: and they did unto them likewise.*
>
> *"But last of all, he sent unto them his son, saying, They will reverence my son.*
>
> *"But when the husbandmen saw the son, they said among themselves, This is the heir; come, let us kill him, and let us seize on his inheritance. And they caught him, and cast him out of the vineyard, and slew him.*
>
> *"When the lord therefore of the vineyard cometh, what will he do to those husbandmen?*
>
> *"They say unto him, He will miserably destroy those wicked men, and will let out his vineyard unto other*

husbandmen, which will render him the fruits in their seasons.

"Jesus saith unto them, Did ye never read in the Scriptures, The stone which the builders rejected, the same is become the head of the corner: this is the Lord's doing, and it is marvelous in our eyes?

"Therefore say I unto you, the kingdom of God shall be taken from you, and given to a nation bringing forth the fruits thereof. And whosoever shall fall on this stone shall be broken: but on whomsoever it shall fall it will grind him to powder.

"And when the chief priests and Pharisees had heard his parables, they perceived that he spake of them."

"He that hath ears to hear, let him hear."

TWO

Secrets of the Antichrist Revealed

"For nothing is secret, that shall not be made manifest; neither any thing hid, that shall not be known and come abroad."

—*Luke 8:17*

"There is scarcely an event in modern Europe that cannot be traced back to the Jews. We Jews are today nothing else but the world's seducers, its destroyers, its incendiaries, its executioners."

—Oscar Levy, Jewish Scholar, in the Preface to *The World Significance of the Russian Revolution* (1920)

The Destroyer is at hand. He is among us. He will be revealed to the Saints soon. We cannot know the exact date of his ascension to global power and authority, but we can know and discern the season. *II Thessalonians 2* prophesies he will rise up only after a great *"falling away"* from the Truth. Is there anyone who doubts that such a falling away has occurred and is still in progress?

I have thoroughly researched the scriptures and written this book so that you will know of his coming. In *Daniel 12:10* we are told that, "In the last days the wicked will do wickedly, and none of the wicked shall understand" what is happening all around them. But, say the scriptures, "The wise shall understand."

A Sure Word of Prophecy

Who is wise but the person who trusts and has faith in God and in His Word? Yes, we have a *"sure word of prophecy" (II Peter 1:19)* to guide and direct our paths.

The Bible has much to reveal to you and me about the Antichrist, the Son of Perdition, the man given the evil number 666. However, the world cannot understand the secrets revealed in God's Word. The people of the world, regardless of their university training and their supposed "scholarly" knowledge, understand little about the deep things of the God-inspired intellect.

Having taught on the faculties of three great universities, amid thousands of learned professors and world-class researchers, I have often lamented, *"God, give me just one man or woman, with or without worldly knowledge, who assiduously reads, studies, and knows the Word of God. Let me, I plead, be a student of such a godly person."*

"Here am I Lord. Send Me!"

In 1986, when I was 42-years old, I felt an insatiable, burning desire to study the things of God and to unravel the mysteries of scripture. It was as if, like the prophet in the Old Testament,

I could hear God's voice, saying, *"Who will go for us? Whom can we send?"* I cried out, *"Here am I, Lord. Send Me!"*

That is when my life took a definite turn for the better. Though highly successful, having years of experience as an Air Force officer, serving across the globe, earning two college degrees, teaching at three great universities, and authoring over a dozen acclaimed secular books, I was consumed with the urge to serve God in full-time Ministry. I was especially interested in discovering the secrets of the coming of the wicked Antichrist. I believe that my entire life to that point had been a preparation for my calling into this Ministry.

The Secrets Revealed In This Book

Today, some thirty years later, I am pleased to present to you, my dear friends in Christ, this book. ***The Destroyer: The Antichrist Is At Hand*** is for the believer who yearns for the truth. Jesus Christ told us to "knock and the door shall be opened... Seek and ye shall find."

> *"For nothing is secret, that shall not be made manifest; neither any thing hid, that shall not be known and come abroad."*
>
> *—Luke 8:17*

> *"If ye continue in my word, then are ye my disciples indeed; And ye shall know the truth, and the truth shall make you free."*
>
> *—John 8:31-32*

Please note Jesus' powerful words, *"the truth shall make you free."* If you are reading this book and do not yet know Jesus Christ as Lord and Saviour, my prayer is that the prophecies explained here will convince you of the utterly supreme power of Bible prophecy. The Bible's prophecies contradict what much of the world erroneously believes to be "truth." I pray that after seeing these contradictions and being fully convinced of the correctness of the prophecies, you will be drawn to the side of Jesus Christ.

Openly Declared Secrets of Prophecy

In these pages, I endeavor to reveal prophetic secrets and truth that, in many cases, have never before been known. Yet, they are openly found in the Holy Bible. And if you are a sincere student of God's Word, I am convinced that God wants you to know and to understand these things. You will therefore discover in this book *55 Proofs in the Holy Bible*, including these eighteen momentous truths:

- ❑ The *name* of the Antichrist
- ❑ The *nation* of the Antichrist
- ❑ The *unholy city* where the Antichrist rises up
- ❑ The *religion* of the Antichrist
- ❑ The *Babylonian* connection of the Antichrist
- ❑ The *source* that empowers the Antichrist
- ❑ The *number* of the name of the Antichrist
- ❑ The *blasphemy* of the Antichrist
- ❑ The *mark* of the Antichrist
- ❑ The *color* used by the Antichrist which signifies blood and death
- ❑ The *motto* of the Antichrist
- ❑ The *Beast* that propels the Antichrist to power
- ❑ The hated *enemy* of the Antichrist
- ❑ The *wealth and greed* of the Antichrist and his people
- ❑ The *demonic nature and personality* of the Antichrist
- ❑ The extent of the *global empire* of the Antichrist
- ❑ God's *judgment* on the Antichrist

❑ The *final destiny* of the Antichrist

To Illustrate His Glory

You will find these revelations in no other book. I have thoroughly searched the scriptures and asked God to open up these things to illustrate His glory. What I have discovered is that the Bible has more than amply covered this important subject. Here are just a few of the many revelations opened up:

1. The Antichrist will be a Jew and his religion a form of kabbalistic Judaism.
2. He will rise up, seize power, and reign from his unholy capital city, Jerusalem.
3. He will be empowered by the Great Red Dragon, the Serpent, known as the Devil or Satan.
4. His mark is the witch's hexagram, the ancient six-pointed star of Jewry.
5. His number, 666, will be revered and cherished by the Jews as a holy number with "messianic potential."
6. He will rule the nations and be recognized by Christians as Gog, from the land of Magog.
7. With the subservience of proxy nations, he will establish military rule, extinguish Christianity, and establish a supremely immoral government and a decadent, depraved culture.
8. He will declare himself "God" and claim to be above all that are called "gods." He will thus blaspheme Jesus Christ, the true and only God, and the host of heaven.
9. He will require all on earth to receive his mark, or his name, or the number of his name either in their right hand or in their forehead. All who refuse this sign in their bodies will be beheaded.

10. At the peak of his influence and power, the Antichrist will be judged by God, convicted and be cast into a fiery hell for all eternity. This is the ultimate fate of the man of sin, the lawless one who rebels against the Almighty.

A Jew Will Rule the World

Now, the sure prophetic truth that the Antichrist shall be a Jew and that his religion will be Judaic and kabbalistic flies in the face of almost every so-called Christian Bible teacher of today. So let me discuss this amazing turn of events.

One of the pleasures of my being head of a Christian Ministry is reading and writing books. I have personally authored over 50 titles and have read countless volumes. People often send me books, thinking I can use the information therein for my Ministry study. I appreciate that.

Recently, I received in the mail a book entitled, *A Jew Will Rule the World.* Just seeing that title and the cover gave me about all the information I needed to know about this book. It was exactly like 15 or other similar titles I had read on this subject. All are fables written by Christian dispensationalists, all these books go over and over the same topics and cover essentially the same material.

Basically, the typical plot goes this way. Jesus died on the cross and temporarily went to heaven. He left the Jews here on earth as His Chosen People and has carefully kept and guided them for about two millennia. The Jews have their own Covenant and they despise Jesus and reject Him as Messiah. But Jesus doesn't really mind their hatred of Him and continues to bless their rebellious nation. Indeed, anybody that blesses the Jews, Jesus will bless and whoever does not, Jesus will curse.

Finally, the books claim that, in His own time, Jesus comes back to earth. He punishes all evildoers—except, of course, the Jews—and He saves all the Jews and sets them up as rulers of the Gentiles and of earth. He Himself is the Chief Ruler and sits on an earthly throne in a rebuilt Temple in Jerusalem, His world capital. Jesus also saves a number of Gentiles, although they, the Gentiles, are definitely second class citizens of earth.

And thus, these books end with the man Jesus, a Jew, on the throne, the collective Jews being supreme as rulers, and the gentiles helping out the Jews as required. It's all a very neat, tidy system with Jesus and the Jews reigning over all.

Naturally, I left out some details, but you can figure those out for yourself. Essentially, these books cover the same territory, exalting the Jews as "little gods" and as future "blossoming saints."

Oh, I almost forgot the most interesting part. Note that, in this myth, Jesus, say the authors, is a Jew. He dies and goes to heaven bodily as a Jew, he will return as a Jew, and he will reign as chief ruler of all the earth as a Jew, still in a Jewish body. It is, after all, a Jew World being prophesied.

These kinds of books keep coming out, one after another. *The Destroyer—The Antichrist Is At Hand* is far different. This book is biblical. It stands by the Bible and trusts the Bible. It is not predicated on the Jews being idolized and turned into "little gods."

What About an Islamic Antichrist?

In past eras, it was speculated that the antichrist could be Hitler, Mussolini, Stalin, or the head of the European Community. Lately, a number of books have come out erroneously declaring the soon coming of the *Islamic Antichrist*. Whoever is most in vogue is usually fingered to be the likely "antichrist." It's sort of a pin-the-tail on the donkey type of game.

But this depiction of God's prophecy of the antichrist as a

Muslim is a grave error. In the evangelical Christian community today are many such errors. This error is often promoted by the Jews. The Church has always been rife with the myths and fables of the Jews, who seek thereby to pollute and destroy the Word of God and to artificially enhance the image of Jews and Judaism.

In *I Timothy 1:4*, Paul told us, do not *"give heed to fables and endless genealogies."* In chapter 4 of the same book, Paul advised us to *"refuse profane and old wives' fables."* Then, in *Titus 1:14*, Paul again reiterates the danger of believing in Jewish myths and fables. He speaks of "deceivers" and cautions the Christian to not *"give heed to Jewish fables, and commandments of men, that turn from the truth."*

The Destroyer: The Antichrist Is At Hand is not based either on Moslem theories or on Zionist myths or on fables invented by Jews and Judaizer Christians. It is a solid book which points exclusively to the scriptures. My goal has been to ever keep an eye on the scriptures so that readers will have a proper—that is, a scriptural—understanding of the last days and of the antichrist.

We will, in this book, be taking a close look at the history of the Jews and of their religion, a Satan-based religion that fully supports the antichrist and accentuates his demonic behavior and mind-set. But first, we turn our attention to the *Destroyer* himself, the Antichrist. We will discover that the Destroyer is the guide and leader for a special race and nation of people. This race is known in history as the "People of the Serpent." At its apex is the *Destroyer,* and those who comprise the elite of this small band of satanic miscreants are themselves self-identified as *we, the destroyers*.

THREE

The Jewish Messiah

"Israel does not just believe that it has an exclusive divine mission. This people, race and nation has become its own Messiah, putting itself in the place of God. Self-worship is at the core of their psyche and world program."

—Hugh Akins
Synagogue Rising

"And the serpent said...Ye shall not surely die... ye shall be as gods"

—*Genesis 3:4-5*

As we shall see, the Jewish people has for centuries yearned for a Messiah to come, to rule over Israel and the entire world. However, the Jewish conception of Messiah is far different than the Messiah as envisioned by Christians.

In the Jewish view, the Messiah will be a man. He will only be "god" in the sense that according to the Talmud and Kabbalah, all Jews are gods. The Jewish Messiah will be the

New King David, an anointed ruler whose military talents and diplomatic achievements enable him to lead all nations on earth. He will lead a New World Order. He will not be a Christ and certainly not the Son of God.

How will he rise to power? The Jews are only a small and insignificant piece of overall humanity. Of some seven billion inhabitants on earth, there are no more than nineteen million Jews. However, the Jewish nation is comprised of Jews residing in a number of powerful nations across the globe. In the U.S., the two percent of the population of the Jews are very wealthy. They control the larger corporations, the media, the education system, publishing and entertainment, and especially have influence in politics. No one can become President of the United States without the imprimatur of the Jews. The same is true in Europe and in South America.

Basically, Jews rule the world by proxy. Wars in the Middle East and elsewhere only occur with Jewish high approval.

What we have is a real situation in which the Jews are the richest and most powerful cult on the face of the planet. Their banking empire is huge and their ownership of the high tech industry—Facebook, Microsoft, Dell, Oracle, Yahoo, etc.—puts the Jew in the drivers seat of world affairs.

The Serpent as Managing Director

The Kabbalah is very explicit in its teaching that it is the Serpent who oversees the activities of the Jews around the world. From the abyss, the bottomless pit, he watches over the People of the Serpent and guides their paths. It is the Serpent who is their King and Lord.

Many Jews, even the most devout, pray to the Serpent and to Satan, or Lucifer. They picture him not as an enemy or as adversary, but as a friend and helper.

According to Judaism, Satan has little initiatory power. Rabbi Eliezer Danzinger of the Chabad group, says that he is simply "a spiritual entity that faithfully carries out its divinely assigned task of trying to seduce people to stumble."

That is his divine job. In fact, the Talmud says, "All that Satan does, he does for the sake of heaven."

"Ultimately," says Rabbi Danzinger, "all Jews have a portion in the world to come." Jews do not go to hell, and Satan's purifying process excludes the Jew. So, in effect, Satan, the Serpent, is the Jews' holy companion.

The kabbalists believe that the whole world exists within the circle of the Serpent. Thus, they envision the Oroboros, a mighty snake encircling all the world and grasping its tail within its mouth. They see the Jewish people as the divine People of the Serpent. The Jews are within the belly of the Serpent.

As the cycles of history occur, the Jew travels the circumference of the circle, descending down into a pit, or abyss. There, he goes through a number of life cycles, called transmigration. The Serpent oversees these life cycles.

The Oroboros, the serpent, or Leviathan, encircling the globe. He represents the Jewish people which historically are called by many the "People of the Serpent."

Eventually, the Jew rises up out of the pit, moving upward towards divinity and self-godhood. Finally, he reaches the kabbalistic level of Kether, or Crown. At this stage, he has descended into the material world, the abyss, and emerged upward out of the abyss. He has become god. Harmony, *Ordo Ab Chao*, is achieved.

The Jews are thus taught by kabbalistic rabbis that collectively they shall be "God." It is the Serpent (whom the Jews refer to as the "Holy Serpent") who is to be thanked. He has been the life-long helper of the Jews. Through Serpent Power *(The Force)* they have risen and collectively are God and shall now reign over the Gentiles and be kings on earth.

The Day of Purification

However, the role of the Holy Serpent requires that, having driven the Jews to the pinnacle of global sovereignty, this sovereignty is only complete when he has completed his tasks. These include what is called the *Day of Purification*, when all Gentiles must choose. Will they renounce their idols (Jesus, Mohammed, etc.) and agree to serve the Jewish effendi (Masters) as slaves, or perish? Serve or die, this is the choice.

The Holy Serpent will also produce the Jew who will become the Patriarch, the Despot-King of Earth. He will heap together (taken from the Gentiles) all the treasures of earth—the gold, silver, precious gems, land and other properties.

The Despot-King will, according to the *Protocols of the Learned Elders of Zion*, have become the Sovereign Lord of all the World. But the Jews collectively control this benevolent monarch.

At this point, having accomplished the divine tasks assigned him, the Serpent, or Satan, will declare the Jews to *collectively* be their own *"Messiah,"* co-rulers with the New King David. He will then depart them, aiming for other worlds and stars, to perform other missions.

We can, then, picture the Jews as the capstone of a Great Pyramid. They shall sit as "God" and potentate of their own planet, needing no other deity or agent to lead them. Collectively, the Jews are Messiah, the New King David being their chosen director or king.

Thus the Talmud Shall Be Fulfilled

In 1888, Baruch Levy sent a letter to fellow Jew, Karl Marx (*La Revue de Paris*, p. 54, June 1, 1928). The letter envisions the fulfillment of the Talmud and the coming future world of the Jews. He writes:

> "The governments of people will pass with the formation of the universal republic effortlessly into the hands of the Israelites... Then the personal property of the rulers will be suppressed by the rulers of the Jewish race, who will everywhere govern... Then the promise of the

Baruch Levy, in 1888, sent a letter to Karl Marx assuring him of the eventual triumph of the Jewish people over the whole world. Marx went on to become the Father of Communism with his many writings.

> Talmud will be fulfilled, and when the time of the Messiah has come, the Jews will have the goods of all peoples of the world in their possession."

As for the future role of the Jewish race, Levy stated:

> "The Jewish people as a whole shall be their own Messiah... Its Kingdom over the universe is obtained through the suppression of frontiers... In this new organization of mankind, the Sons of Israel, who at present are scattered over the entire earth's surface, will all be of the same race and of the same traditional culture without, however, forming another nationality...successful in laying upon the masses of workers a permanent leadership by Jews."

The Jews diminish the authority of the Holy Bible, substituting for its words the passages in the *Babylonian Talmud*, which were written long ago by Jewish rabbis. The Kabbalah, too, is a series of books written since the Middle Ages by Jewish rabbis. Therefore, the religion of the Jews, based on the Talmud and the Kabbalah, comprise the "traditions of the elders." God had no part in writing these books, which the Orthodox Jews scrupulously obey.

It does not surprise us, then, that the Jews are exalted in the Talmud and Kabbalah as a divine species, as a collective "God" on earth. It is, moreover, the Sanhedrin, a group of rabbis, who claim to be the authority in interpreting these holy books.

Judaism is an incestuous sex cult pretending to be a religion. It is invented by the Jews, puts the Jews on a pedestal as gods-in-becoming, and actually places the Serpent in the chief leadership role. No external God will do for the Jews. They don't want to obey a so-called deity, in heaven or on earth. Collectively, they shall be gods of a man-made universe, free of the shackles of the real God, while dumbly being subject to the Serpent, which is Satan the Dragon.

The Jews are self-Chosen. Oh sure, Messiah shall come. He will be the New Moses, the new King David, richer than King Solomon. But He will not be God. He will, instead, serve the Jews as one of them, a god among gods, as taught to them by their true leader and guide, the Holy Serpent.

Rabbi David Cooper explains that when the Jew speaks of the "coming of Messiah," he is referring to the "coming of messianic consciousness" which all advanced Jews will have in common.

Rabbi Yitzchak Ginsburgh, author of *What You Need to Know About the Kabbalah*, speaks of the doctrine of the famous Jewish sage, Baál Shem Tov. According to this doctrine, the Shekinah (divine feminine) presence, a divine spark or energy force, is found in advanced Jews. A combination of these divine sparks (*collectively*, the Jewish people) make up the sanctified elite. They will comprise the leadership of the future Jewish Utopia and will collectively usher in the Messianic Age.

The Children of Pride

Let's face it. Any group of people who believe in a self-generated literature that claims they are the Chosen, of a special and unique blood type which makes them the Super Race is logically insane. Anyone who claims I am divine, but all others (the Goyim) are mere beasts and animals, is not only narcissistic but demonically bent and hopelessly out of their mind. The book of Job calls them the "children of pride."

All who support these looney-tunes—and regretfully, I

include many evangelical Christians—have fallen into the clutches of Satan. They are in the grip of the Strong Delusion. They are prepared and ready to believe in the evil of the Mystery of Iniquity.

Their darkened hearts will enthusiastically embrace the Antichrist, who comes in the form of the Jews' New King David but who seizes power and rules over all as the Son of Perdition. He is the one prophesied in *II Thessalonians 2*, who will declare himself not only God, but above all other gods. By the time he is on the scene and grabs authority for himself, his disciples, having fallen from the truth, will be caught up in a tidal wave of lying miracles and strong delusions. They will believe in the Lie.

FOUR

The Gospel of Christ and The Gospel of Antichrist

> "It would seem as if the Gospel of Christ and the gospel of antichrist were destined to originate among the same people."
>
> —Sir Winston Churchill, in *The Illustrated Sunday Herald* (London, February 8, 1920)

In 1920, before becoming Prime Minister of Great Britain, Sir Winston Churchill wrote an important article for *The Illustrated Sunday Herald* newspaper in London. He noted the revolutionary activity of the Jews throughout modern history, from the days of "Spartacus" (code name of Adam Weishaupt, founder of the Illuminati, in Bavaria) to the recent, 1917, overthrow of the giant Russian Empire by Lenin, Trotsky, and other communist Jews. He wrote of the inhuman savagery and brutality of the Jews in Russia and stated:

"It may well be that this same astounding race may at the present time be in the actual process of producing another system of morals and philosophy as malevolent as Christianity was benevolent... It would seem as if the Gospel of Christ and the gospel of antichrist were destined to originate among the same people."

ILLUSTRATED SUNDAY HERALD, FEBRUARY 8, 1920. Page 5.

ZIONISM versus BOLSHEVISM.

A STRUGGLE FOR THE SOUL OF THE JEWISH PEOPLE.

By the Rt. Hon. WINSTON S. CHURCHILL.

SOME people like Jews and some do not; but no thoughtful man can doubt the fact that they are beyond all question the most formidable and the most remarkable race which has ever appeared in the world.

Disraeli, the Jew Prime Minister of England, and Leader of the Conservative Party, who was always true to his race and proud of his origin, said on a well-known occasion: "The Lord deals with the nations as the nations deal with the Jews." Certainly when we look at the miserable state of Russia, where of all countries in the world the Jews were the most cruelly treated, and contrast it with the fortunes of our own country, which seems to have been so providentially preserved amid the awful perils of these times, we must admit that nothing that has since happened in the history of the world has falsified the truth of Disraeli's confident assertion.

Good and Bad Jews.

The conflict between good and evil which proceeds unceasingly in the breast of man nowhere reaches such an intensity as in the Jewish race. The dual nature of mankind is nowhere more strongly or more terribly exemplified. We owe to the Jews in the Christian revelation a system of ethics which, even if it were entirely separated from the supernatural, would be incomparably the most precious possession of mankind, worth

Mr. Churchill inspecting his old regiment, the 4th Hussars, at Aldershot last week.

The National Russian Jews, in spite of the disabilities under which they have suffered, have managed to play an honourable and useful part in the national life even of Russia. As bankers and industrialists they have

like Bukharin or Lunacharski cannot be compared with the power of Trotsky, or of Zinovieff, the Dictator of the Red Citadel (Petrograd), or of Krassin or Radek—all Jews. In the Soviet institutions the predominance of Jews is even

people, most of whom are themselves sufferers from the revolutionary régime. It becomes, therefore, specially important to foster and develop any strongly-marked Jewish movement which leads directly away from these fatal associations. And it is here that Zionism has such a deep significance for the whole world at the present time.

A Home for the Jews.

Zionism offers the third sphere to the political conceptions of the Jewish race. In violent contrast to international communism, it presents to the Jew a national idea of a commanding character. It has fallen to the British Government, as the result of the conquest of Palestine, to have the opportunity and the responsibility of securing for the Jewish race all over the world a home and a centre of national life. The statesmanship and historic sense of Mr. Balfour were prompt to seize this opportunity. Declarations have been made which have irrevocably decided the policy of Great Britain. The fiery energies of Dr. Weissmann, the leader, for practical purposes, of the Zionist project, backed by many of the most prominent British Jews, and supported by the full authority of Lord Allenby, are all directed to achieving the success of this inspiring movement.

Of course, Palestine is far too small to accommodate more than a fraction of the Jewish race, nor do the majority of national

Sir Winston Churchill, in 1920, wrote a perceptive news article in which he stated, "It would seem as if the Gospel of Christ and the gospel of antichrist were destined to originate among the same people."

Already reports were coming in to Britain of the horror of the Red Terror, overseen and perpetrated by the Jews of Russia and of the world. Many Jews, hearing of the Jewish overthrow of the Czar, rushed from their home country to Russia to help their fellow Jews seize power and administer the government.

They firmly believed that Russia was only the first of many republics sure to fall like dominos as the Jews successfully built their long-awaited Jewish Utopia, the World Kingdom.

The first law passed by the new communist legislature was Lenin's *Anti-Semitism Act*, which made it a crime to criticize or even to speak negatively about the Jews. Soviet gulags were built, executions began, and blood flowed as Christianity was banished and all freedoms curtailed. Solzhenitsyn, in his sobering book, *Two Hundred Years Together*, states that over seventy percent of the commandants of the gulags were Jewish rabbis. The head of the murderous Cheka, the predecessor to the KGB, was a Jew and over ninety percent of the government leadership were Jews.

In America, the leading Rabbi, Stephen Wise, proudly hailed the Jewish triumph in Russia. *"Communism is Jewish!,"* said a prideful Rabbi Wise.

The Jewish-controlled media in the U.S.A. and in Europe managed to cover-up the fact that Karl Marx, from whom the communist philosophy sprang, was a Jew, and that almost all the revolutionaries were Jews.

Stalin's Jews

In 2006, in a surprising article in *YNET News*, a widely read Jewish publication, columnist Sever Plocker, a Jew, wrote a revealing article entitled "Stalin's Jews" in which he explained the purging, death, and destruction meted out during the communist era. *"We must not forget,"* wrote Plocker, *"that some of the greatest murderers of modern times were Jewish."*

Lenin and Trosky, the two Jewish revolutionaries who overthrew the Czar and took power in Russia (renamed the U.S.S.R.—Union of Soviet Socialist Republics) were, indeed, "among the greatest murderers of modern times." Solzhenitsyn says that some 66,000,000 were massacred in the decades of Jewish rule in Russia. This stunning figure gives one an idea of how utterly devastating will be the regime of the Jewish antichrist when he ascends to global rule in the last days.

Only the servants of Satan would be so violent and psychopathic as to engineer and execute the savagery displayed by the communists. That Karl Marx, the originator of Communism, was a stooge of Satan has been proven. In his excellent book, *Marx and Satan*, Richard Wurmbrand presents documentation of Marx's satanic involvement. He was also a Zionist. Communism was a way to reach all the goals of Zionism while pretending to liberate mankind. In fact, in his writings, Marx claimed that the Jews were already *emancipated* and that Christians were emancipated to the extent that they had become "Judaized."

Marx hated God and dreamed of destroying Him. In his poem, *Invocation of One in Despair*, he slammed God for holding him back.

"So a god has snatched from me my all
In the curse and rack of destiny
All his worlds are gone beyond recall
Nothing but revenge is left to me.
I shall build my throne high overhead,
Cold, tremendous shall its summit be.
For its bulwark—superstitious dread.
For its Marshall—blackest agony.
Who looks upon it with a healthy eye,
Shall turn back, deathly pale and dumb,

Clutched by blind and chill mortality,
May his happiness prepare its tomb."

In another poem, Marx railed against God and angrily claimed that he was equal to the creator:

"Then I will be able to walk triumphantly,
Like a god, through the ruins of their kingdom.

Every word of mine is fire and action.
My breast is equal to that of the Creator."

But the true goal of Marx was to be an annihilator, a destroyer. He craved to be able to destroy the entire universe. Listen to these dark Satanic words from his poem, *Oulanem*:

"If there is a Something which devours,
I'll leap within it, though I bring the
world to ruins—
The world which bulks between me and the abyss
I will smash to pieces with my enduring curses

I'll throw my arms around its harsh reality
Embracing me, the world will dumbly pass away
And then sink down to utter nothingness,
Perished, with no existence—that
would be really living."

These verses could only come from the devil. No wonder Marx's disciple, Lenin, as head of Soviet Russia cried out repeatedly, *"More blood! More blood!"* The Red Terror continued inexorably on its path of obliteration.

Then, in his last days, his mind ravaged by syphilis, Lenin

was wheeled in his chair to a balcony from which he would howl non-stop like a wolf.

The Samson Option

The Jews have a fascination with destroying civilization. They are truly the *"annihilators."* If they cannot possess the jewels and treasures of the world, no one else will. That is their satanic attitude. This attitude practically destroyed the Russian Empire.

The Atomic Age was enthusiastically embraced by the Jews. It was the brainchild of New York City Jews to give President Roosevelt the *Manhattan Project*. Roosevelt in turn, put Oppenheimer, a Jewish scientist, in charge of developing the first nuclear bomb. That bomb was used at Hiroshima and Nagasaki in Japan at the insistence of Morgenthau and other Jews. The Jews later stole America's nuclear plans and gave them, first to Soviet Russia and later to Israel.

J. Robert Oppenheimer, Jew and head of the Manhattan Project, which gave the world the atomic bomb. Oppenheimer later wrote that, upon viewing the first testing of the atomic bomb, his thoughts were a quote from the Hindu scriptures, the *Bhagavad Gita*, "Now I have become the Destroyer of worlds."

Today, Israel is one of the few nations to have the atomic bomb and the missiles to use it. Israel has even threatened to take down the entire world if they are threatened. In 2003, Israeli professor and military historian Martin Van Creveld said that the Samson Option would be used if need be.

> "Speaking during an interview which was published in Jerusalem Friday, Professor Martin Van Creveld said Israel had the capability of hitting most European capitals with nuclear weapons.
>
> "We possess several hundred atomic warheads and rockets and can launch these at targets in all directions, perhaps even at Rome. Most European capitals are targets of our Air Force...
>
> "Asked if he was worried about Israel becoming a rogue nation...Creveld quoted former Israel Defense Minister Moshe Dayan who said, 'Israel must be like a mad dog, too dangerous to bother.'
>
> "'We have the capability to take the world down with us,' said the Professor. 'And I assure you that this will happen before Israel goes under.'"

Professor Martin Van Creveld sounds like a mad man, does he not? But, remember, Satan has gotten into and infected the minds of the Christless Jews. In their Talmud and in the books of the Kabbalah, the rabbis are told that Jews are a separate, higher species, a race of god men. As such, they expect to be reborn and to reign over this planet. Satan may well be urging the Jewish leaders to kill and murder on a genocidal scale, persuading them that they will be reincarnated upward in the new World, the Jewish Utopia, where they will rule over the remaining Goyim.

The Serpent People of Magic and Satan

The Jews have since the days of Khazaria been known as the Serpent People. To Christians, this connotes great evil, but to the Jews, it means superiority in wisdom and cunning. In his outstanding 1,100 page book, *Judaism Discovered*, Michael Hoffman II explains:

> "The core of Judaism, like the core of Gnosticism and Egyptian Hermeticism, is magic, the manipulation of the universe, contra God's creation, i.e. against nature. Gershom Scholem, Professor of Kabbalah at Hebrew University, wrote that Kabbalah embraced a great deal of 'black magic...a wide realm of demonology and various forms of sorcery that were designed to disrupt the natural order of things.'"

The Jews once were in the evil clutches of Egyptian and the Pharonic religion. They worshipped at the altar of the Star god of the Egyptian pantheon of deities. Hoffman writes: "The rabbis hold Egypt in awe as a magical powerhouse. Pharonic Egypt is the model, root, and source for Talmudic and Kabbalistic priestcraft."

Judaism, then, is a satanic cult posing as a religion. And in Jewish theological schools, the Old Testament and its Torah are de-emphasized. Considered only a fount of myths and legends, the Rabbis claim to find secret, hidden knowledge even in the very letter of the Hebrew alphabet. They also assert that magic is contained in numbers, calling this occult science,

"Gematria."

Jesus, of course, warned of this wicked cult when he referred, in Revelation, to the *"Synagogue of Satan."* Do not think for a moment that the entity and people whom Jesus forewarned about as the Synagogue of Satan, full of blasphemy, would not be able to produce the heinously evil antichrist. In fact, Judaism is the perfect vehicle for such a monstrous personality.

Whereas, Christianity is the Church of Jesus Christ and involves the life and teaching of Christ, i.e. the Gospel, Judaism and its practice of kabbalism and talmudism is the very Gospel of Antichrist.

FIVE

Judaism: A Covenant With Death and An Agreement with Hell

"And I saw an angel come down from heaven, having the key of the bottomless pit and a great chain in his hand. And he laid hold on the dragon, that old serpent, which is the Devil, and Satan, and bound him a thousand years, And cast him into the bottomless pit, and shut him up, and set a seal upon him, that he should deceive the nations no more, till the thousand years should be fulfilled: and after that he must be loosed a little season."

—*Revelation 20:1-3*

"Babylonian Judaism is a religion of demons."

—Edward Hendrie
Solving the Mystery of Babylon the Great

Have you ever asked a Christian pastor to tell you something about Judaism—about its doctrines, its rituals, its conception of heaven and God? I have, and invariably the pastor tells me that Judaism can be found in the Old Testament. The many pastors to whom I addressed the question say that Jews are monotheistic, that they believe in one God in Heaven. They also explained that the Jews must follow all the laws in the Old Testament that were given to Moses. They naturally mentioned the Ten Commandments and say that Jews believe strongly in living a holy life, stress love and charity toward others, and pray often to their one God.

In sum, virtually every Christian pastor you talk to believes that the Jews are simply Old Testament believers, and that is about it. But, of course, in reality, Jewish rabbis rarely, if ever read, study or teach from the Old Testament.

Their laws do not come from it but are found in a set of volumes called *The Babylonian Talmud*, and it is a compilation of commentaries not written by God but by the rabbis themselves.

The Babylonian Talmud has 613 laws the righteous Jews must obey. Probably few Jews can even remember such a complex and long set of laws. Many of the laws are obscene and ridiculous. Some are blatantly unrighteous and cruel. Jesus criticized the Talmudic laws as not of God but rather as *"man-made."* In all the Talmud is up to 63 volumes in length, and impossible for a man to read and comprehend.

Consider some of the actual laws found in the Babylonian Talmud. Is this not a prescription for evil, not good? Is this not the perfect religion for the Antichrist to wield and require? Is there any religion in the world more wicked and mischievous in its rules and doctrines?

- When a grownup man has intercourse with a young girl less than three years old, no damage is done. She remains a virgin *(Kethuboth 11a-11b)*.
- It is acceptable for a 9-year old boy to have sex with a grown-up woman *(Abodah Zarah 36b-37a)*.
- A man may commit sodomy with a boy of less than nine-years old and no guilt is incurred *(Sanhedrin 55b-55a)*.
- Jesus corrupted morals and dishonored self *(Sanhedrin 107b)*.
- Do not associate with Gentiles *(Abodah Zarah 22a)*.
- Christians who worship Jesus are idolaters *(Zohar I, 28b)*.
- Non-Jew souls go to hell *(Rasch Haschanach 116a)*.
- Books of Christians must be burned *(Schabbath 116a)*.
- To strike a Jew is the same as slapping God *(Sanhedrin 58b)*.
- Gentiles are not human, but are beasts *(Emek Hammelech 23d)*.
- Forbidden to teach Gentiles a trade *(Iore Daea 154,2)*.
- Permitted to deceive Christians *(Babha Kama 113b)*.
- Jew may lie and perjure to condemn a Christian *(Babha Kama 113a)*.
- Jews may cheat Christians *(Babha Kama 113b)*.
- Do not save lives of Christians in danger *(Hikkoth Akum X, 1)*.
- Even the best of Gentiles—kill *(Abhodah Zarab 26b)*.
- Make no agreements and show no mercy to

Christians *(Hikkoth Akum X, 1)*.

- ❑ Acceptable to lie to Christians *(Kallah 1b)*.

These are only a small portion of the laws a Jew is expected to obey. The Babylonian Talmud is considered superior to the Holy Bible and because it is so wicked, a Jew may be killed who teaches it to a Gentile, According to the Babylonian Talmud, even God Himself goes to the knowledgeable rabbi for spiritual advice.

Supplanting and Replacing the Old Testament

In the Jewish religion, there is also yet another set of books taught, called the Kabbalah, which include many of Judaism's teachings, including its advocacy of superstitions about black magic, sorcery, astrology, demons, gods and goddesses, demi-gods, talismans, amulets, charms, and so forth. These books, written by rabbinical teachers (Jesus called them "Scribes"), have, in Judaism, supplanted and replaced the Old Testament. The Old Testament is given short thrift by the rabbis, who insist that their occult methods be used to "interpret" what they claim are the *hidden* doctrines concealed or imbedded in the actual words of the Old Testament. For Jews, then, the Kabbalah interprets the Scriptures and it is studied in place of the Scriptures.

A Religion of Bigotry, Hatred, Deceit, and Worse

What you find in the *real* religion of Judaism, as contrasted with the average Christian's almost totally incorrect view is that Judaism is a religion of bigotry, hatred, deceit, money, and lust, populated with a plethora of gods, goddesses, goblins and devils. Worst of all, the researcher and investigator discovers, to his horror, that Judaism is a dark religion that praises evil.

And not just your garden variety of evil, either. I mean downright filthy, brutal, monstrous evil.

Although many evil and vulgar and distasteful teachings and practices are found in the Jews' Babylonian Talmud, it is the Kabbalah that presents us with the most thorough and developed *system* of degenerate evil.

Magic and Occult Mysticism

Edward Hendrie, a Christian attorney and researcher of Judaism and Zionist philosophies, reports in his book, *911: Enemies Foreign and Domestic*, that, "Magic and occult mysticism run throughout the Kabbalah." He cites a number of Jewish authorities who confirm his own findings:

> "Judith Weill, a professor of Jewish mysticism, stated that magic is deeply rooted in Jewish religion, but the Jews are reticent to acknowledge it... Gersham Scholem, Professor of Kabbalah at Hebrew University in Jerusalem, admitted that the Cabala contains a great deal of black magic and sorcery, which he explained involves the powers of devils to disrupt the natural order of things...Professor Scholem also stated that there are devils who are in submission to the Talmud. In the Cabala these devils are called "Shedim Yehuda 'im."

As might be expected in a set of occult books instructing the reader on how to practice black magic and sorcery, according to Hendrie, "The Kabbalah, like the Talmud, graphically blasphemes Jesus. For example, in *Zohar-111 (2882a)*, the Kabbalah refers to Jesus as a dog who resides among filth and vermin. Blasphemy, as grotesquely a sin as it is, is only one of many depravities we find openly displayed in the Kabbalah.

In Satan is a Divine Spark

The holy person, says the Kabbalah, is not necessarily the person who does good and who thinks pure and wholesome thoughts. He who embraces evil—even maximum evil—can be equally rewarded and blessed. Thus, the entire spectrum of good and evil is a 360° circle. The more good one does, the more he ascends, but then he must balance this good by descending an appropriate degree. Hell and Heaven are each depicted as both descending and ascending. The integrated person is the most holy for he has integrated and woven both evil and good into his life.

Rabbi David Cooper, in *God is A Verb: Kabbalah and the Practice of Mystical Judaism*, alludes to the value of evil when he remarks that evil can be redeemed, and that divinity can be found in unlikely places:

> "The lesson is that even the heart of Satan has a divine spark; even the heart of evil yearns to be redeemed. This is important because...our job is not to...eradicate evil, but to search out its spark of holiness. Our job is not to destroy but to build."

In essence, the task of the Jew is to build up the kingdom of Satan on earth. That kingdom will be one in which the Jews take possession of all the world's wealth and rule over the Gentile nations. It is no wonder that both the Jews and their companions in sin, the Freemasons, lay claim to being "The Builders."

Contrast with Christians

The Christian Scriptures, however, present us with a stark contrast to this Judaic doctrine that evil is good. Jesus said he came to "destroy the works of the devil." Indeed, Paul says in the Scriptures that if any man not build on a strong foundation, he builds in vain, and Jesus is that strong and steady foundation. The New Testament affirms the incompatibility of good and evil and counsels the believer in Christ to "abstain from all appearance of evil" *(I Thessalonians 5:22)*. Jesus in His Lord's Prayer, prayed, "Deliver us from evil."

The Old Testament, too, contradicts the Jews' assertion that evil is good and that to become most holy a person must taste and immerse himself in both good and evil We read in *Isaiah 5:20*: "Woe to them that call evil good and good evil." Indeed, we find God constantly admonishing His people to refrain from evil:

> *"Turn ye, turn ye from your evil way."*
> *—Ezekiel 33; 11*

> *"And turn every man from his evil way."*
> *—Jeremiah 26: 3*

> *"Ye that love the Lord, hate evil."*
> *—Psalms 97: 10*

> *"Hate the evil, and love the good."*
> *—Amos 5: 15*

Whereas the Jews work diligently to combine and embrace both good and evil, teaching that the holy person is hereby elevated to perfection and divinity, the Scriptures teach that this is a doctrine from hell:

> *"Ye cannot drink the cup of the Lord and the cup of devils: Ye cannot be partakers of the Lord's table and of the table of devils.*

In their feast of Sukkot, the Jews honor the Lord of Sukkot, the Supreme God of the Sephiroth (Tree of Life), whose symbol is both the crown, representing majesty and glory, and the skull, representing death. Their Kabbalah prescribes a great feast on the holy day or Sukkot, when the Jews shall attain their kingdom on earth. At this feast, or banquet, the Jews teach that the Holy Serpent, Leviathan, shall be consumed, eaten. Thus this Sukkot feast will be the "table of devils" and the Jews are the "partakers." Having rejected Christ Jesus as Lord, their Lord becomes Satan, that old Serpent, the Devil.

Only a religion based on the principles of Satan could be so vile and repulsive as to boldly claim that a man can be redeemed and made holy by committing evil. Who but the Devil's crass disciples could invent so utterly malignant a doctrine?

A New Paradigm: Uplift Evil

Rabbi Cooper, who spent eight years studying the Kabbalah in Jerusalem, points out that Judaism encourages Jews to appreciate the divine qualities of evil:

> "The mystical teaching of (Judaism's) Baal Shem Tov... presents us with a new paradigm. It says that evil has a divine nature within it. As the *Zohar* describes, 'there is no sphere of the Other Side (evil) that entirely lacks some streak of light from the Side of holiness' *(Zohar II: 69 a, b)*. Rather than destroy it (evil), our task is to uplift it."

Baal Shem Tov, which means, "Master of the Divine Name," is a title given to Rabbi Yisrael ben Eliezer, the rabbinical sage who founded the Hasidic Jewish sect. According to Eliezer, Jews must work to uplift evil and search and find the divine light concealed in the depths of the darkness.

No wonder Jesus so vigorously opposed and attacked the man-made religious traditions of the Jews. He saw that the Pharisees (a sect of Judaic believers that the *Encyclopedia Judaica* says is today's Orthodox Judaism) were little more than evangelists for their father, Satan.

Jesus wasted no words in declaring:

> *"Woe unto you scribes, (religious scholars) and Pharisees, hypocrites! For ye compass sea and land to make one proselyte, and when he is made, ye make him twofold the child of hell than yourselves."*
> *—Matthew 23:15*

Of course, the Jews, being hypocrites, accused Jesus of being "Beelzebub, the prince of devils." Today, they continue to blaspheme the holy name of Jesus. It is not surprising, then, that they worship Satan and seek to "uplift" and redeem evil. It was the Apostle Paul who said that Satan comes disguised as an "angel of light" and his disciples as "ministers of righteousness" *(II Corinthians 11: 14-15)*.

Review of the Kabbalah

Few Christian pastors or religious teachers have ever taken the time to study the complex Jewish Kabbalah, although it is central to the faith of many Jews, and its principles and concepts are woven into the tapestry of the entire field of the Judaic belief system. One pastor who has studied the Kabbalah and its doctrines is John Torell, a good friend of mine, who is founder of European-American Evangelistic Crusades. In that organization's publication, *The Dove* (Winter 1993), Torrell reported on his extensive research into the teachings of Kabbalism.

In examining the Ten Sefirot of the Kabbalistic Tree of Life, which he notes are claimed to be the ten "emanations" of the Godhead, Pastor Torell centers in on the Jews' doctrine of distinct male and female deities. The Father or male, is given the name *"Hokhmah"* and the mother, or female, is called *Binah*. Now there is yet another male form of God exalted as even greater than these two. He is mysterious, unknowable, and unattainable to man by direct means.

Many Jewish rabbis insist this supreme male deity, named *Ein Sof* is immanent (that is, present or dispersed) in all things, all matter, visible and invisible. Others say that *Ein Sof* is a unified being, but invisible, being neither of spirit nor material substance. This compares with the Christian view—expressed in the New Testament—that "God is a spirit."

Torell explains that in the rabbinical teachings, the highest God, *Ein Sof*, being detached and ineffable to man, has "withdrawn himself into himself." He is in the wilderness. This created a vacuum in his own structure, a "bottomless pit," or "abyss." This terrible abyss is called the "kelipah" by the Jews. The kelipah, or bottomless pit is a hellish place inhabited by countless evil spirits and demonic entities of various forms and natures.

Ask a Christian pastor, celebrity, or evangelist, whom do the Jews worship; that is, who is their God, and he will undoubtedly answer, "Why, the Jews believe in the great I AM, the God of the Old Testament, the same God worshiped by we Christians."

Present that same pastor with evidence of the many gods and goddesses taught by the rabbis and even given names in their Kabbalah and Tree of Life, and watch the eyes of the poor, pitiful Christian pastor gloss over. Pastors are woefully ignorant and most have absolutely not a shred of knowledge as to the awful truth of the Judaic godhead.

That is why the rabbis must chuckle with glee when they are invited by dumbed-down, ignorant Christian pastors and leaders to pray and speak at so-called "interfaith" gatherings and worship services. The rabbis pray and invoke devils and the stupid Christians mistakenly think they are calling on the God of Moses, Jacob, Elijah, Isaac, and Jeremiah!

The Holy Serpent Ushers in the Jewish Utopia

All Jews long for the coming of the Jewish Messiah. In fact, the serpent beast, Leviathan, is recognized as this coming Messiah

When he, the Holy Serpent comes, then will come the "Jewish Utopia," a glorious time of heaven on earth, with the divine Jews empowered by the Serpent to overcome and rule the world. This auspicious occasion will be inaugurated by a great Feast, or Banquet, during which the Jews will eat of His flesh and drink of His blood. There will be the "Real Presence" and Eucharist of the Holy Serpent. This doctrine is similar to that of the Roman Catholic Church in which, in the Eucharist, a wafer of unleavened bread, is consecrated as the actual body of Jesus Christ.

Thus will the Jews collectively ascend to the throne of world power and hegemony. Through Holy Serpent power, Leviathan rises in victory to represent the whole "Community of Israel." The Jews will become Messiah. By the serpent's incorporating its incomparable supernatural power, the Jewish Nation will be a beacon for all humanity, the "Light of the World."

The Holy Serpent will, the Jews believe, appoint one of

their own to be the New King David. Though a man, he will be a great leader, leading the divine Jews forward into paradise. He will oversee the Day of Purification, during which the Gentiles will be judged and most killed by beheading.

The one whom the Jews will honor and revere as their New King David will be the very one whom the Christians recognize as the incarnation of Satan on earth: The prophesied Son of Perdition, the Antichrist.

God Power Through Both Good and Evil

However, as I mentioned, according to the Kabbalah's teachings, the Jews themselves must create the conditions which make possible the ascension of the Holy Serpent from the bottomless pit where it is imprisoned. They can do this in two ways—either they can destroy all evil on planet earth and make it perfect and whole; or second, the Jews are to destroy all good on earth and render it wholly evil.

The rabbis teach that *perfection* occurs through the integration and balance of good and evil. The candidate for perfection sinks deep into evil and is immersed in sin. Then and only then can he or she ascend into the light. The path is circular and along the way he partakes of both the left hand *(evil)* and the right hand *(good)* until the circle is complete.

The Oroboros, the Holy Serpent, represents this Sabbatian process in that the Serpent, in a route of circumambulating, moves from light into darkness and returns to the light. Through destruction and creation the creature becomes whole, the circle is complete.

The Original Blessing—The Gift of Lucifer

Thus, the divine Jew transcends the light and dark spheres and is beyond good and evil. The act of Lucifer in enticing Eve and seducing her in the Garden is a creative, or generative act. It is, in fact, as Barbara Marx Hubbard teaches in her eye-opening book, *The Original Blessing*, a positive act. Yes, Eve did the right thing, says Hubbard, and the kabbalists fully agree. In taking a bite out of the forbidden fruit, in disobeying Jehovah and giving in to Lucifer, the Serpent, Eve set mankind on the path of divinity.

Adam and Eve, in eating the forbidden fruit, are believed to have achieved gnosis, they knew both good *and* evil. And, as God (the plural *Elohim*) well knew, the two were therefore on the threshold of divinity.

The kabbalists maintain that this was something that the cruel and oppressive Jehovah God did not want—for Adam and Eve to become integrated and be part of the Elohim—so he banished them from the Garden. However, through the doctrines and practice of Kabbalah, it is believed that man allegorically can *return* to the Garden—he/she can become as gods. Only through gnosis, experiencing and *knowing* the fullness of both good and evil, can this be accomplished. The Lie through which the serpent seduced Eve and Adam has today became the holy doctrine of the Jews.

Edward Hendrie writes that the Cabalistic Jews firmly believe they must commit sin and do the maximum of evil, and when the world is sufficiently full of evil, their hoped for Deity will ascend out of the bottomless pit and empower the Jews to reign and rule:

> "This Cabalistic religion is grounded in the commission of sins in order to bring about the ascension of their Messiah, the "holy serpent," out of the bottomless pit to make 'her' appearance on earth. These Jews believe that only by breaking the laws of God can they serve their god."

But, Hendrie adds, "Do not think that Jews are ignorant of the fact that Satan is god of their religion." He further elaborates:

> "Harold Wallace Rosenthal, Administrative Assistant to (Jewish) United States Senator from New York Jacob K. Javits, in a 1976 interview with Walter White, Jr., stated: 'Most Jews do not like to admit it, but our god is Lucifer.'" (*The Hidden Tyranny*, by Walter White, Jr.).

These modern-day Pharisees, Hendrie notes, go to great lengths not only to sin themselves but also to lead others to sin as they serve their evil god, Satan.

The Holy Serpent Prophesied in Revelation

That the whole world is to eventually be seduced into accepting the Jewish dogma of the Holy Serpent is prophesied in the book of *Revelation*. Mystery, Babylon the Great is none other than the Jews and their religion. Described as the Mother of Harlots, who sits upon the beast, she (the Jews religion and dogma) sucks into her vortex of evil all the nations on earth:

> *"Come hither, I will shew unto thee the judgment of the great whore...with whom the kings of the earth have committed fornication...*
>
> *And the angel said unto me...I will tell thee of the mystery of the woman, and of the beast that carrieth her: The beast...shall ascend out of the bottomless pit, and go into perdition."*
>
> *—Revelation 17: 2,7-8*

The Jews teach that the beast that ascends out of the bottomless pit is their Holy Serpent. It is He that gives the Jews and the last days of the House of Israel supernatural power to reign as divine humans over the nations. But the Word of God *(Revelation 17)* refutes this unholy lie. The beast and all those who worship him shall "go into perdition—and everlasting burning hell."

The Plan: Saturate Earth with Evil

What the Jews intend to do, then, to fulfill the Plan in the Kabbalah for world domination and a ruling earthly Kingdom of the Jews, is to saturate the whole earth with evil. In doing so, they are invoking the symbolical "God of Forces" who is to come as prophesied by the prophet Daniel. Their lust for acquisition of money will be instrumental in this quest. "The love of money is the root of all evil," the Bible says *(I Timothy 10)*.

To their satanic god, the God of Forces, Daniel prophesied, the Jews will heap great treasures. Money begets evil and fuels sin, and the whole world is to become a planet of evil. It is through maximum evil that the Jews' Holy Serpent shall be empowered to conquer.

Hendrie comments, that in this terrible kabbalistic doctrine, that of committing maximum evil, the Devil will realize his final objectives:

> "Surely Satan has an end in mind for construction of such a sinister religious doctrine. He does, and it is nothing short of the subjugation of all men under the dictatorial rule of his antichrist! He uses the escalating sin and crime in society to bring about more government regulation and control of the masses..."

John Torell, in his lengthy study of kabbalism and the Jews' religion, amplifies the findings of Hendrie:

> "This evil doctrine can also be seen in the Talmud, where incest, fornication, adultery, etc. are promoted as virtues and something to be desired. It is difficult for the Gentile world to fully comprehend what is happening in the Jewish netherworld of conspiracy unless they understand the nature of Cabalistic Judaism. It is a religion based on the promotion, propagation, and commission of sin as a means to world domination." ("Showdown in Jerusalem," *The Dove*, winter 1995)

The Holy Serpent Ascends From the Bottomless Pit

Now let us recap these strange, rather bizarre teachings of the kabbalist Jews. Their holy books tell us that the ineffable and distant "God" *(Ein Sof)* has withdrawn into himself and left a void, a bottomless pit (the "kelipah") in which the Jews' deity, the Holy Serpent, Leviathan, is imprisoned along with countless evil spirits and demonic entities. These many spirits and entities the Jews do not recognize as demonic, but as instruments that help attain perfection and godhood.

There, in this dark and terrible abyss, the Holy Serpent strives to free itself. It will eventually emerge into the material world, earth, through the power generated by both the good works and by the sins and evil committed by Jews here on earth. Ascending out of the bottomless pit and coming forth up on the surface of earth, thus emerging from the bottomless pit, the serpent and its divine followers, the Jews, shall conquer and shall reign supreme as the "Light of the World."

As Christians we have read of all this before; in fact, it is found in the New Testament's prophetic book of *Revelation 9: 1-11*. So let us go now to *Revelation* where we discover that, indeed, these momentous truths are set forth, though with a different perspective and result. *Revelation* provides us with a complete understanding of this key doctrinal teaching of Kabbalah:

> *"And the fifth angel sounded, and I saw a star fall from heaven unto the earth: and to him was given the key of the bottomless pit.*
>
> *"And he opened the bottomless pit; and there arose a smoke out of the pit, as the smoke of a great furnace; and the sun and the air were darkened by reason of the smoke of the pit.*
>
> *"And there came out of the smoke locusts upon the earth: and unto them was given power, as the scorpions of the earth have power.*
>
> *"And it was commanded them that they should not hurt the grass of the earth, neither any green thing, neither any tree; but only those men which have not the seal of God in their foreheads.*
>
> *"And to them it was given that they should not kill them, but that they should be tormented five months: and their torment was as the torment of a scorpion, when he striketh a man.*
>
> *"And in those days shall men seek death, and shall not find it; and shall desire to die, and death shall*

flee from them.

"And the shapes of the locusts were like unto horses prepared unto battle; and on their heads were as it were crowns like gold, and their faces were as the faces of men.

"And they had hair as the hair of women, and their teeth were as the teeth of lions.

"And they had breastplates, as it were breastplates of iron; and the sound of their wings was as the sound of chariots of many horses running to battle.

"And they had tails like unto scorpions, and there were stings in their tails: and their power was to hurt men five months.

"And they had a king over them, which is the angel of the bottomless pit, whose name in the Hebrew tongue is Abaddon, but in the Greek tongue hath his name Apollyon."

—Revelation 9: 1-11

So here, in *Revelation 9*, we find the "bottomless pit" of the Jewish Kabbalah. It is, exactly as the Kabbalah teaches, the hellish residence of demonic things—supernatural "scorpions," "locusts" and other frightening creatures. According to the Scriptures they have a "king over them," whose name in the Hebrew language is "Abaddon."

Note the striking parallels of the passages in *Revelation* with the Kabbalah's teaching. According to the kabbalistic rabbis, their divine Holy Serpent has fallen into a bottomless pit and is surrounded by demonic creatures and entities. This Holy Serpent deity eventually ascends and emerges out of the bottomless pit where it was confined and goes on to anoint the empowering "Messiah" of the Jews. It is this Holy Serpent, say the kabbalists, whose spirit enters and possesses the body and mind of the Jews' new "King David." Through serpent power, the Kabbalah doctrine says, the Jews will conquer the entire world and be as divine kings and queens on earth, lording over the Gentiles.

The Parallels Continue

We have yet another amazing correspondence between the Jews' doctrine and the prophecies in *Revelation 20*, where we are told that Satan, "that old serpent," is bound for a thousand years in the bottomless pit and then is "loosed a little season":

> *"And I saw an angel come down from heaven, having the key of the bottomless pit and a great chain in his hand.*
>
> *"And he laid hold on the dragon, that old serpent, which is the Devil, and Satan, and bound him a thousand years,*
>
> *"And cast him into the bottomless pit, and shut him up, and set a seal upon him, that he should deceive the nations no more, till the thousand years should be fulfilled: and after that he must be loosed a little season."*

So the serpent bound up or confined in the bottomless pit is the Devil, or Satan. And whom do the Jews say is this divine reptile? The Jews call their deity "Leviathan" and honor this serpent deity as their overshadowing spiritual Messiah. The books of *Job* and *Isaiah* in the Old Testament identify Leviathan as the "piercing serpent" and say that the true God of the Bible and of Christianity will in the end of days destroy wicked Leviathan.

In *Revelation 13*, Leviathan is described symbolically as the beast that rises up from the sea. We compare this with the teachings of the Kabbalah, which depict the Jewish Messiah, their great Holy Serpent, as ascending, or rising up from the "bottomless pit."

Finally, we see in *Revelation 9* that the devils that reside in the bottomless pit have a king over them, "whose name in the Hebrew tongue is Abaddon."

The Jews claim no knowledge of the book of *Revelation*, yet their holy books exalt Abaddon as an emanation of God, to be honored as a deity. But, hold on: even the Old Testament teaches that Abaddon is the Devil and that:

> *"Hell is naked before him, and destruction hath no covering."*
>
> *—Job 26:6*

Who is Abaddon?

Christians know from studying the prophetic book of *Revelation* that *"Abaddon"* is a name for Satan. The Hebrew word, Abaddon means *"The Destroyer."* But remember, in Judaism, God is both creator and destroyer; he is a composite of both good *and* evil. Therefore, we would expect Judaism to teach that Abaddon is yet another name for their divine "God." And in fact, among the ten deities (Sefirots) of the kabbalistic Tree of Life, we find the name *"Nezah,"* which the Kabbalah reveals is actually the same as "Abaddon."

Thus, Glenn Barken, a teacher of Kabbalah, in an online course, *Angelology 112—Who Is Abaddon?*, writes that Abaddon is the positive entity that "assists the human spirit across the Abyss on its path toward divinity." One reaches the supreme God by bridging this final obstacle.

Abaddon *(Nezah)*, says Barken, is actually the archangel of the abyss, or pit.

In my studies both of the "Christian" cult of the Jehovah's Witnesses and Freemasonry, I discovered how Satan is using these false, kabbalistic systems to exalt the divine archangel Abaddon. In the Masonic Lodge, a secret password is used called the *Sacred Word*. The Sacred *Word* is *Abaddon.*

Meanwhile one of the most revered figures in the Jehovah's Witnesses religion Judge Joseph Rutherford, beginning as far back as 1930, taught that Abaddon is actually a synonym for Jesus!

Abaddon, Leviathan, Nezah—these descriptions are all of the same creature, who comes disguised in numerous guises. That creature, whom the Jews call the Holy Serpent, the Scriptures call the "dragon...that old serpent, called the Devil, and Satan" *(Revelation 12: 9)*. In this same prophetic passage in Revelation, we are told that this is the one "which deceiveth the whole world: he was cast out into the earth, and his angels were cast out with him."

Power in Bible Prophecy

What power we find demonstrated in God's prophetic books! Imagine, *Revelation 12* and *13* gives us a marvelously clear picture of Satan and his dark angels as they ascend from the bottomless pit and ravage the earth doing their diabolical work of destruction. And in the Jewish Kabbalah is a mirror copy of this same series of events. Who can deny that the Jews know exactly whom it is they serve: Satan! Their symbols, their holy books, seem to have been produced direct from plagiarizing the book of *Revelation*.

It is amusing, is it not, that the Jews are adamant in insisting that the *Protocols of the Learned Elders of Zion* are a forgery. Yet, in the *Protocols* we find that their holy books of Kabbalah are parroted from the New Testament's book of *Revelation*. Similar parallels are discovered in the books of *Job, Isaiah*, and in the four gospels. The difference is that the Scriptures identify these positive Jewish "gods" as devils.

Apparently, the devil just cannot escape his pitiful destiny, and neither can the rebellious, Christ-hating, Christ-killing Jews! It is God's decision that these usurpers of truth, these world bandits and troublemakers, must follow to a "T" the pattern of prophecy laid out and written down some 2,000 years ago in the books of the Holy Bible. The Jews cannot escape their fate. Their leaders long ago tragically made a "Covenant with death" and an "Agreement with hell." Leviathan, the muse of Satan, will make sure they comply with the deal that they struck. And God shall oversee and guarantee the matter.

That the Jews did make a covenant and agreement with death and hell shall become even more clear in the succeeding chapters. We look next at the man whom the Jews will someday honor and revere as their great leader and New King David. We Christians know him as antichrist, the evil one possessed and incarnated by the Devil himself.

SIX

Dress Rehearsals for the Antichrist

"Then if any man shall say unto you, Lo, here is Christ, or there; believe it not. For there shall arise false Christs, and false prophets, and shall shew great signs and wonders; insomuch that, if it were possible, they shall deceive the very elect. Behold, I have told you before."

—Jesus Christ
Matthew 24:23-25

In October of 2015, in Israel, highly respected Rabbi Chizkiyahu Mishkovsky, spiritual advisor for several religious learning centers, told a gathering that, according to an esteemed rabbinical authority, Rabbi Chaim Kanievsky, the arrival of the Messiah is close. Rabbi Kanievsky pleaded, "Go out and tell the people, we are in the most critical hours for the nation of Israel. We are on the threshold of the Messiah, and the Messiah is standing just outside the door."

Rabbi Kanievsky directed that younger rabbis take a loudspeaker and "go around the whole country to tell the people. Yell it out loud!"

Jewish history is replete with similar examples of Jewish rabbis and rebellious leaders claiming to be on the threshold of the Messianic Age; sometimes, the Jews have cried out, "The Messiah is here!"

It is as if, having rejected and crucified the true Messiah, Jesus Christ, the deluded Jews will settle for almost anyone. Jesus said, "I am come in my Father's name, and ye receive me not: if another shall come in his own name, him ye will receive" *(John 5:43)*.

The Bar Kokhba, One of Many False Messiahs

In the year AD 132, a man named *Simon Bar Kokhba* arose and declared himself the Messiah of the Jews. The Jews flocked to this militant and many called him, the "Son of the Star." Simon promised the Jews independence from Rome and the free and full worship of the Judaic faith. He and his followers commenced to war against the Roman legions, killing many soldiers and inciting Jewish rebellion that spread to many neighboring nations.

Bar Kokhba and the Jewish revolutionaries, believing God was on their side, did not hesitate to commit horrible atrocities. In city after city, they savaged locals, and their acts were horrible and brutal.

Like deadly psychopaths, they cornered Christians and Greeks alike, smashing them with stones, tearing out their entrails, gouging out eyes, and eating raw flesh. It was hell on earth everywhere that Bar Kokhba was celebrated as the Jewish Messiah.

It took Hadrian and the Romans two and a half years to fully gather their forces and to begin a campaign to wipe out

Bar Kokhba and his rebels. But village by village the legions of Rome conquered, though Bar Kokhba rebels fought like wild men possessed. Eventually, the Romans overcame the so-called "Messiah of the Jews."

Simon Bar Kokhba, who claimed to be "Messiah of the Jews"

The Romans slaughtered some 580,000 Jewish citizens and banished Jews from their capital city of Jerusalem.

Because he failed in his lofty Messianic ambitions, today Bar Kokhba is referred to as "Ben-Kusiba" in the Talmud, to indicate that he was a false messiah.

Throughout the Roman Empire, Gentiles spoke harshly of the Bar Kokhba revolt and its monstrous crimes against innocent citizens. This revolt, being repugnant, was the primary cause of anti-Semitism in the early centuries after Jesus.

Since the days of Bar Kokhba, others have come forth, claiming to be the Jewish Messiah and rousing many followers.

"Communism is Judaism"—The World Revolution

In 1917, with the Jews in control of the U.S.S.R. and the advent of world communism, Jews across the globe began to speculate that the Jewish Messianic Age was drawing near. By 1939, the Jewish communists had butchered and savaged tens of millions of Christians in Russia. The Jews saw the Marxist paradise as the cornerstone of their Judaic New World Order.

In New York City, in San Francisco, in Chicago, and in the capitals of Europe, Jews everywhere celebrated what they viewed as the threshold of world victory.

One leader in the 30s was Rabbi Harry Waton, a Bolshevik communist propagandist who despised America, his home country, and was gloriously happy that the Jews were killing and marauding in former Gentile-led nations. Waton was certain that the Jews would win their war against the Nazis and Fascists. Remember, this was 1939, two years before America entered the conflict on the side of the Jews.

In his inflammatory 1939 book, *A Program for the Jews and an Answer to All Anti-Semites*, Rabbi Waton outlined his beliefs about the Jews conquering the Gentile nations and establishing the Messianic World Republic. Here are some of the statements found in that book:

> "The communist soul is the soul of Judaism... In the Russian revolution the triumph of communism was the triumph of Judaism.
>
> "It is not an accident that Judaism gave birth to Marxism, and it is not an accident that the Jews readily took up Marxism; all this was in perfect accord with the progress of Judaism and the Jews.
>
> "It is with these (communist) spiritual weapons that the Jews will conquer the world and the human race. The races and the nations will cheerfully submit to the spiritual power of Judaism, and all will become Jews.
>
> "This is the kingdom of the Jews, of all Jews...

> This is the predetermined destiny of mankind, of all mankind, without exception... The Jewish people are eternal.
>
> "The only immortality there is for the Jew is the immortality in the Jewish people. Each Jew continues to live in the Jewish people, and he will continue to live so long as the Jewish people will live.
>
> "When we disregard the scientific cloak of Marxism, we see that in essence it is nothing else than religion."

Waton understood that Marxism and communism were not atheistic. That was, as he wrote, only a "scientific cloak," a disguise intended to deceive the masses. No, communism was definitely a religion. It proposed to destroy religion but, in fact, was itself religion:

> "The communists are against religion, and they

Rabbi Harry Waton was a Jewish supremacist who believed that communism would propel Jews to global domination.

> seek to destroy religion; yet, when we look deeper into the nature of communism, we see that is essentially nothing else than a religion."

That is why, Waton explained, that, "communism is Judaism." The Jews in charge of the revolution in Russia and in other countries knew theirs was a religious mission. Their goal was to force everyone to jettison their existing religion, thus, to be emancipated. This destruction would follow in due time in their becoming "Jews." Either they would convert—or they would die.

Judaism, wrote Waton, was the *only* historic and moral religion. It would survive while all others fell. This was the arc of world history, its inevitability. "The Jews have a right to subordinate to themselves the rest of mankind The Jews will become the masters over the whole earth."

Communism Meets Goals of Judaism

Communism (*aka* Judaism) still today insists it will eventually rule the whole world. This, claim its Marxist teachers, is "inevitable." Even the abject economic and social failure of Soviet Communism in the 1980s does not deter their spirit. This is because communism is actually a mirror copy of Judaism.

As far back as 1883, *The Jewish World* carried an article which confidently predicted the eventual global victory of Judaism:

> "The great ideal of Judaism is that the whole world should be imbued with Jewish teachings, and that in a universal Brotherhood of nations—a greater Judaism in fact—all the separate races and religions shall disappear."

As one learned rabbi told me, "We Jews do believe in *Ordo Ab Chao* (Order out of Chaos)." "In the process of time," he said, "we shall actually consume, or digest the chaos and force order upon the world."

The Jewish rabbis intend to *dechristianize* the world, to rid the globe of the last vestiges of Christ Jesus, to utterly destroy Gentile culture and to create *Tikkun Olam*, the Jewish Utopia. Maurice Samuel, in his assertive book, *You Gentiles*, states: "We Jews, we the destroyers, will remain destroyers forever."

Genocide in Palestine—Israel Reborn

David Ben Gurion, a Pole and a Jew, who served as the first Prime Minister of modern Israel, believed that eventually the Jews would rule as gods over all. In speaking of a coming Jewish Utopia, he wrote:

> "Jerusalem aspires to become the spiritual center of the world... In Jerusalem, the United Nations will build a Shrine of the Prophets to serve the federated union of all continents; this will be the scene of the Supreme Court of mankind, to settle all controversies...as prophesied by Isaiah." (quoted in *Look* magazine, January 16, 1962).

Ben Gurion was a Jewish supremacist who oversaw the genocide and ethnic cleansing of tens of thousands of Palestinian natives. He wanted to deport all Palestinians whom he didn't massacre. A rabid supporter of Marxist-Leninism, David Ben Gurion stated, "Our policy must be the unity of the human race," with, of course, the Jews as the leaders and gods on earth.

"I believe in our moral and intellectual superiority," Ben

David Ben Gurion, first Prime Minister of Israel (1948), on the 50 shekl note.

Gurion boasted. He also believed in the bloody reign of the Jews.

With evil men such as David Ben Gurion in leadership in Israel since 1948, many Jews have believed that the time of Messiah is at hand. But almost seven decades have passed and there still is no Jewish Messiah.

The Lubavitcher Rebbe—Is He the Messiah?

Some Jews today believe that a rabbi who lived and died in 1994 was and is the Messiah. Lubavitcher Rabbi Mendel Schneerson, from Brooklyn, New York, who was head of the Chabad Lubavitch, the largest and most successful of Orthodox Jew movements, is the man they finger as the Messiah. Schneerson was promoter of the Noahide Laws, an important set of laws in the Talmud which explain the servant role to be played by Gentiles in the coming Messianic future of Israel and the world.

When Schneerson passed away in 1994, many of his followers said he would be resurrected and be the Messiah.

Rabbi Mendel Schneerson, acclaimed to be the Messiah of the Jews, died in 1994.

Schneerson preached a rigid kabbalistic message, emphasizing God's feminine side as the Shekinah Presence. He shared the belief that the Jews are Chosen and are a divine species. The Jews, he said, are truly their own Messiah. Therefore, he taught that, "The Messiah has already come. All that is necessary is for people to open their eyes in order to greet him."

According to Schneerson, "The non-Jewish soul comes from three satanic spheres." Adolf Hitler, he stated, was "divine punishment" for Jews who had assimilated with Gentiles and did not accept the Chabad view of radical Orthodox Judaism.

The Sabbateans and Their Messiah, Sabbatai Zevi

Sabbatai Zevi was born in Smyrna, in Greece, a city in present-day Turkey in 1626. The name "Sabbatai" literally means the planet Saturn, and in Jewish tradition, Saturn, sixth planet from the sun, is linked to the advent of the Messiah.

At age 22, in 1648, Sabbatai, a young teacher of the Kabbalah, suddenly declared to his followers that he was the Messiah redeemer. Ten years later, he persuaded a well-known rabbi that he was, indeed, the true Messiah. His fame as Messiah began to grow among the people and other rabbis.

Superstitious Christians had begun to tout the year 1666 as the potential year of the end of the world (because it included three sixes). The Jews, hearing of this, began to adopt the same date for the coming of the Jewish Messiah, and so Sabbatai's claims grew.

Then, the famous kabbalist rabbi, Nathan of Gaza, announced his belief in Sabbatai as Messiah, and declared him the "risen Elijah." He declared that Sabbatai would win the world without bloodshed in 1666. Jews everywhere rejoiced, singing out "Long live our King, our Messiah!"

Rabbis and congregations throughout Europe and Asia

Sabbatai Zevi, in 1665

hailed Sabbatai as Messiah. His head swelling over this explosion of popularity, Sabbatai foolishly stated that he would travel to the Moslem capital, where he would remove the Sultan's crown from his head. He, Sabbatai, would then assume the role as head of the Ottoman Empire.

This worried the Sultan, and when Sabbatai arrived in Constantinople, the Sultan had him arrested and jailed. Sabbatai lingered in prison for many months before being given an ultimatum. Either convert to Islam or die. Sabbatai converted.

The Sultan, pleased with his decision, awarded Sabbatai a sum of money and granted him the title *Mehmed* (effendi), or doorkeeper. About 200 other Jews, Sabbatai's local supporters, also chose conversion. Sabbatai exclaimed, "God has made me an Ishmaelite." The new converts took on the name *Donmeh* (converts).

Sabbatai attempted to convince his wide following throughout the world that his conversion to Islam was ordained by God. He claimed it was necessary to stealthily convert the Moslems to Judaism. But the masses, disillusioned, did not believe him, and most of his disappointed followers left the ranks. Still, quite a few Jews remained loyal and to this day, one can find remnants—numbering about 100,000—of the Donmeh in Turkey and throughout the Middle East.

Sabbataism

One of the lasting doctrines of Sabbatai Zevi is called *Sabbataism*. Zevi, as the erstwhile "Messiah," had many strange doctrines and this was one of them. This evil doctrine actually was very popular among the Jews in the 17th century and now has become a widespread belief and facet of 21st century Judaism. It is held by many Jews.

In Sabbataism it is taught that there are two ways that a

Jew can become righteous and holy, earning a place in the future world. First, he can do many wonderful and humanitarian works of charity and kindness. This is the pious route to eternal glory. Or, the Jew can seek to do terrible deeds of treachery and evil. Either way, the Jew is doing mikvahs (works) which are attributed to him. He earns karmic credits for either the good or the bad.

Thus, today's Jew believes that he must be very good or very bad. This doctrine is obviously a wicked one, but it is nevertheless embraced and the term "Sabbataism" now has a peculiar meaning for Jews. Some who practice this doctrine attempt to be especially cruel and sinful, convinced this bad conduct earns great rewards.

SEVEN

Jesus Took the Kingdom From the Jews

"Therefore say I unto you, The kingdom of God shall be taken from you, and given to a nation bringing forth the fruits thereof."
—*Matthew 21:43*

Today, there are millions of evangelical Christians who are convinced by Zionist propaganda that they must assist the Jews in building up the earthly nation of Israel. They say that *Genesis* requires this, that whoever blesses Israel, God will bless, and whoever curses Israel, God will curse.

But, in fact, the way—the only way—to bless Israel is to evangelize the Jews and the modern-day state called "Israel" for Jesus. What greater blessing can there be than to reveal the truth of Jesus Christ?

Believing the Lie, however, many Christians are deceived into thinking that giving money to Israel for hospitals and other projects, or pressuring our Congress to arm Israel with the most sophisticated of military arms and equipment is the pathway to their being blessed. This is tragic.

> *"For other foundation can no man lay than that is laid, which is Jesus Christ."*
>
> *—I Corinthians 3:11*

Many millions also believe that Jews *do not need* Jesus for salvation. The Pope and the Vatican teach this Lie, and many evangelicals buy into it. They say that the Old Covenant of the Jews is still in effect.

The Old Covenant Cannot Save the Jews—It Is Replaced

In fact, the Old Covenant is dead, having been abolished by the New Covenant of Jesus Christ, which, the scriptures say, is a "better covenant" *(Hebrews 8:6-13)*.

> *"But now hath he obtained a more excellent ministry, by how much also he is the mediator of a better covenant, which was established upon better promises.*
>
> *"For if that first covenant had been faultless, then should no place have been sought for the second.*
>
> *"For finding fault with them, he saith, Behold, the days come, saith the Lord, when I will make a new covenant with the house of Israel and with the house of Judah:*
>
> *"Not according to the covenant that I made with their fathers in the day when I took them by the hand to lead them out of the land of Egypt; because*

they continued not in my covenant, and I regarded them not, saith the Lord.

"For this is the covenant that I will make with the house of Israel after those days, saith the Lord; I will put my laws into their mind, and write them in their hearts: and I will be to them a God, and they shall be to me a people:

"And they shall not teach every man his neighbour, and every man his brother, saying, Know the Lord: for all shall know me, from the least to the greatest.

"For I will be merciful to their unrighteousness, and their sins and their iniquities will I remember no more.

"In that he saith, A new covenant, he hath made the first old. Now that which decayeth and waxeth old is ready to vanish away."

What, then, of the Old Covenant, which is replaced by the new and better New Covenant? Note that the New Covenant of Jesus is written on men's hearts. We read this amazing verse in *Hebrews 3:9-14*:

"When your fathers tempted me, proved me, and saw my works forty years.

"Wherefore I was grieved with that generation, and said, They do alway err in their heart; and they have not known my ways.

"So I sware in my wrath, They shall not enter into my rest.

"Take heed, brethren, lest there be in any of you an evil heart of unbelief, in departing from the living God.

"But exhort one another daily, while it is called Today; lest any of you be hardened through the deceitfulness of sin.

"For we are made partakers of Christ, if we hold the beginning of our confidence stedfast unto the end."

The Temple to Be Rebuilt—In Vain

As for the Temple which the Jews say they shall rebuild in all its glory, their efforts are in vain. Paul, in *I Corinthians 3:16*, writes: *"Know ye not that ye are the temple of God, and that the Spirit of God dwelleth in you?"*

In *Acts* we read, *"Howbeit the most High dwelleth not in temples made with hands... HEAVEN IS MY THRONE, AND EARTH IS MY FOOTSTOOL: WHAT HOUSE WILL YE BUILD ME? SAITH THE LORD: OR WHAT IS THE PLACE OF MY REST?"*

The Blessing is Jesus, The Promise is Eternal Life

And the misplaced conviction that whoever blesses the Jews will be blessed by God? The *Blessing* is Jesus! What does it profit a man if he has the whole world but has not Jesus? (see *Matthew 10:39*). This is what we can and must do for the Jews who will receive Him—tell them about Jesus.

But, know this: This same, marvelous blessing is for all nations, all peoples who believe in Jesus as their Lord and

Saviour:

> *"Even as Abraham believed God, and it was accounted to him for righteousness.*
>
> *"Know ye therefore that they which are of faith, the same are the children of Abraham.*
>
> *"And the scripture, foreseeing that God would justify the heathen through faith, preached before the gospel unto Abraham, saying, In thee shall all nations be blessed.*
>
> *"So then they which be of faith are blessed with faithful Abraham."*
>
> *—Galatians 3:6-9*

The Promise

Yes, Jesus will Bless all who believe in Him by giving them the gift of eternal life (*Romans 11:23*). This is His wonderful *promise*. This life is in Jesus Christ our Lord, and He is the very Kingdom of God. Therefore, the Kingdom is not of men. It is not made of buildings, monuments, highways, bricks, or gold, silver, and precious stones. The Kingdom is possessed by He who has Jesus Christ as Lord and Saviour. This is the glory of the Kingdom, and it is for eternity. As Jesus Christ Himself told Roman Governor Pontius Pilate: *"My kingdom is not of this world" (John 18:36)*.

All who have Jesus Christ, who believe in Him, are citizens of this great, eternal Kingdom *(Titus 2:6-7)*. Their nation is Heavenly Zion, and Heavenly Jerusalem is their great city. The redeemed who know Jesus Christ as King are, Peter told us, a royal people, a holy nation, the people of God *(Peter 2:9)*.

Jesus told the Jews: *"Therefore say I unto you, The kingdom of God shall be taken from you, and given to a nation bringing forth the fruits thereof" (Matthew 21:43).*

To what "nation" was Jesus referring? To whom did Jesus give the Kingdom after taking it from the Jews? Peter answers: The holy nation whose citizens are royals and are of Christ Jesus is the Christian nation.

The Jewish Utopia

Opposed to the Kingdom of God, which is of Jesus Christ and is exclusively made up of people of *all* races, is the Kingdom of the Jews. The Jews call it the *Jewish Utopia*. The Kabbalah and the Talmud say that it will become reality with the active help of the Holy Serpent, whom the Jews know as Leviathan.

Let us, for a moment, study this prophesied "Jewish Utopia." We use for reference such textbooks as *The Jewish Encyclopedia* and the books *The Jewish Utopia*, by Rabbi Michael Higger, *The Spirit of Utopia*, by Ernst Bloch, and *Redemption and Utopia*, by Michael Löwy. We also will access the writings of such famous Jewish rabbinical luminaries and scholars as the Rambam, Maimonides, Abraham Ibn Ezra, Rabbeinu Bachya, the Vilna Gaon, Aryeh Kaplan, and the Lubavitcher Rebbe. What follows is the prophetic vision, or plan of the Jews.

The Prophetic Outline of the Jewish Utopia

Once the Jews have their serpentine Utopia, or Paradise, they believe they will be gods of advanced consciousness, and of an entirely different species than the inferior Goyim (gentiles). On the Day of Purification, the Holy Serpent will bring about "creative destruction," the deconstructing of planet Earth. The gentiles will be given a choice—to serve their Jewish masters, or be destroyed. (This is why the Bible names the beast who comes up from the abyss, the pit, "Abaddon." In the Hebrew language, Abaddon means the "destroyer.")

Their Own Messiah

Following the Day of Purification, the Jews shall, they believe, become their own Messiah. The Holy Serpent shall leave them to their own devices; his mission is accomplished.

The Jewish Utopia will be led by a mere King, not a divine God. Jesus, of course, is rejected, and so is the great I AM of the Old Testament. The Kabbalah has demoted I AM and he is now the unfathomable, ineffable and unapproachable, far distant deity called *Ain (or Ein) Sof.* This is perfect for the Jews who will, in the Utopian age, no longer have the Holy Serpent as their overseer and protector. They have no further need of him. They shall be their own Messiah and exercise their divinity as wise men.

As for the Messiah, the new King David, the Man who leads his fellow Jews and the whole world, *The Jewish Encyclopedia* explains:

> "The Messiah is to be a human leader, descended from the Davidic line, who will usher in the Messianic Age. The Messiah will be a very great king. He will achieve great fame, and his reputation...will be even greater than that of King Solomon. His great righteousness and the wonders that he will bring about will cause all peoples to make peace with him and all lands to serve him...it will be a time when the number of wise men will increase...war shall not exist... The Messianic Age will be highlighted by a community of the righteous and dominated by goodness and wisdom... All nations will return to the true

religion and will no longer steal or repress."

"According to Jewish tradition," the *Encyclopedia* continues, this will be an era of "global harmony, a future era of universal peace and brotherhood on earth, and one conducive to the furtherment of the knowledge of the Creator."

The New Religion

Christianity and Islam will be erased from existence. The Noahide Laws forbid the worship of Jesus and of Muhammad. Other religions, too, will be extinguished, as *"all nations will return to the true religion."*

And what is this *"true religion?"* The Jewish sages say that the world will be taught "new knowledge," and that even the pig may be freely eaten in the Messianic Era.

The Antichrist Cometh

Obviously, the Plan for a Jewish Utopia is a dead set-up for the coming of the Antichrist. The Holy Serpent, Satan, will not, as they imagine, simply disappear. And the Davidic King, or Messiah who ushers in the "True Religion" and this heralded "new knowledge" will undoubtedly surprise the Jews with his viciousness and cunning. *He will, in fact, prove to be the Antichrist!*

The demonic world is alive with anticipation over the upcoming Jewish Utopia. The *Tikkun Olam* (mending or restoration) of the world is to be a homecoming of sorts for the Dragon and his chief aide, the Antichrist.

They Have Dug a Pit

As so wisely is stated in *Proverbs 26:27, "Whoso diggeth a pit shall fall therein: and he that rolleth a stone, it will return upon*

The Noahide Laws in the Talmud say that all idolaters, including faithful Christians, will be beheaded during Leviathan's great Day of Purification. Amazingly, this guillotine was erected by Jewish demonstrators in August 2011, in Tel Aviv, Israel.

him."

The Jews, so haughty and proud in their prophecies as to their coming Utopia, have greatly erred. Jesus, wisely warned, *"For by thy words thou shalt be justified, and by thy words thou shalt be condemned" (Matthew 12:37).*

The words of the Jews have condemned them. Theirs shall not be a Utopia but instead, will turn out to be a harrowing and cruel nightmare.

PART II

The Jewish Antichrist

EIGHT

The Jewish Messiah Will be the Antichrist: 55 Proofs in the Holy Bible

The Bible reveals that the coming of Antichrist is the "Mystery of Iniquity," whereas the coming of Jesus our Lord was the "Mystery of Godliness."

Here is absolute and incontrovertible evidence—55 proofs—that the Antichrist, the Mystery of Iniquity, is to be a Jew.

These proofs from the Bible are backed up conversely by the Jews' own holy books—the Babylonian Talmud and the Kabbalah. The Jewish writers of these uniquely Jewish texts say, for example, that the number six hundred, sixty, and six (666) is a holy number imbued with "lofty Messianic potential." Meanwhile, the Bible reveals that the number of the name of the *beast* will be six hundred, sixty, and six (666). In the Bible, this is a wicked number and certainly has *no* "lofty Messianic potential!"

In this and many other cases, we find that the Jews' Talmud

and Kabbalah seem to be drawn like a magnet to *exactly rival* the Bible's descriptions of latter-day evil.

Many may be surprised that the Antichrist will be a Jew. However, it seems that God's wisdom is always confounding man's best judgment. And in this particular matter, the many proofs found here provide us with certitude of this fact.

As Sir Winston Churchill about a century ago noted (*The Illustrated Sunday Herald*, London, February 8, 1920), "It would seem as if the Gospel of Christ and the gospel of antichrist were destined to originate among the same people."

Is this fact not amazing? God is no respecter of persons. Yes, He gave the Kingdom to Israel, to be a shining light and witness to all the world of His glory, power, and majesty. But the Jews, flawed as are all men, failed in that holy mission. They rejected the One whom God had sent and crucified Him on the Cross. Their very words on that solemn, condemning occasion, now return to haunt them:

> *"When Pilate saw that he could prevail nothing, but that rather a tumult was made, he took water, and washed his hands before the multitude, saying, I am innocent of the blood of this just person: see ye to it. Then answered all the people, and said, His blood be on us, and on our children." (Matthew 27:24-25)*

Jesus, merciful as He is, nevertheless continues to shine forth a beacon of salvation even to the belligerent and rebellious Jewish people. In *Mark 16:15-16*, Jesus told his disciples, *"Go ye into all the world, and preach the gospel to every creature. He that believeth and is baptized shall be saved; but he that believeth not shall be damned."*

Regardless, therefore, of the deadly words of the Jews said before Pilate, "Let his blood be on us, and on our children,"

Jews today may be saved.

My plea, then, for the Jews is the same plea that I make for all: Believe in Jesus Christ, and you shall be saved.

55 Proofs:

1

The Antichrist will come in his own name *(Revelation 13:18)*

- ❑ Jesus told the Jews: "I am come in my Father's name, and ye receive me not: if another shall come in his own name, him ye will receive." *(John 5:43)*

- ❑ Jesus is the most hated name in the Jewish world. The Babylonian Talmud, the most sacred holy book of Jewish Law, brands Jesus a "blasphemer," a "magician," and the "son of a whore." It claims that Jesus corrupted Judaism and as punishment is burning in hades for eternity, in fiery feces.

  According to the Talmud, Jesus got what he deserved, and He was duly tried and punished by the Jewish Sanhedrin.

  No other religion on earth is consumed with such hatred and vituperation toward Jesus.

2

The Antichrist's name, counted numerologically, is six hundred, three score, and six (666) *(Revelation 13:18)*.

- ❑ In Judaism, the number 666 is taught to be a good and

holy number.

- ❏ It was Solomon, who, as the King of ancient Israel, defied the true God and worshipped other false deities, including the goddess Ashtoreth. Solomon demanded that the high priests of the Temple annually pay tribute to him 666 talents of gold *(I Kings 10:14)*.

- ❏ One of the first Jewish settlements in modern-day Israel was that of some 100 Ashkenazi Jewish families in the 19th century who arrived and located just outside Jerusalem in a place they called "Meah Shearim." In Jewish gematria, the numerical value of Meah Shearim is 666.

- ❏ In the Kabbalah's *Zohar*, the sage Mosad Hayesod cites the Vilna Gaon's commentary that, *"the number 666 contains hidden within it exalted and lofty messianic potential."*

3 In *Revelation 13* we find two beasts, the first rises from the sea: *"And I stood upon the sand of the sea, and saw a beast rise up out of the sea..."* We read also of this beast, that, *"The dragon gave him his power, and his seat, and great authority."*

Then, in *Revelation 13:11*, a *second beast* comes up, *"out of the earth."* This second beast exercises all the power of the first beast and causes all the world to worship the first beast.

The two evil beasts, one up from the sea, the second rising out of the earth, are both empowered by Satan, the dragon.

- Amazingly, in the Kabbalah, we find two beasts, the first rises out of the sea, which is the watery abyss. The second is in the wilderness, that is, in the earth. The Kabbalah says these two are mirror images of each other. Named "Leviathan" and "Behemoth," these two beasts are the great serpents. The two constitute a dual force of harmony, equilibrium and order. Thus is fulfilled the occult dictum, *"As Above, So Below."* Masonically, this represents *Ordo Ab Chao (Order out of Chaos).*

- These two kabbalistic beasts (serpents) act as one and together they are good and harmonious for the Jews. They work to exalt the Jews to godhood.

---

4 *Revelation 13* says that the second beast will require everyone on earth to take either the mark, or the name, or the number of the beast.

- The *name* of the Jewish nation is Israel but this is also the name of a *man. Jacob*, founder of the nation, was given the spiritual name "Israel" by God (*Genesis 32:28*). So Israel is the name of a man.

- Jacob (or "Israel"), a man of God, had twelve sons and each became leader of one of the twelve tribes of Israel. On his deathbed, Jacob gave a prophecy to each of his sons. The prophecies were generally favorable and promising except for that given to the son, Dan. Dan and his tribe, said Jacob, would prove evil and sinister. Dan would be like an adder, or serpent who hides by the roadside. When the rider and horse come, Dan, the serpent, will strike the heel of the horse so that the rider falls backward. Dan shall bring *judgment* to the people and nation of Israel.

- ❑ In *Numbers 24:17* is yet another important prophecy. We read: *"There shall come a Star out of Jacob, and a Scepter shall rise out of Israel."* The star indicates a king; the scepter is an instrument wielded by the king as a sign of his authority and rule.

Does this prophetic verse apply to Jesus? Indeed it does, for Jesus came from the bloodline of Jacob, and His kingdom and throne is everlasting. However, Jesus' Kingdom is not worldly but is *spiritual* in nature, for flesh and blood cannot enter the Kingdom of Heaven.

But the scriptures also reveal the coming of another Messiah. He will be an imposter, an evil man whom the Jews will accept as their King and confer upon him all authority. He will be the *star* that comes out of Jacob, the descendent of Dan. The six-pointed star will be his shield and sign—the "mark" of his divine throne—he will be a serpent as is his father, Satan. His Kingdom, unlike that of Christ Jesus, will be earthly and be composed of flesh and blood subjects.

To sum up, the bloodline of the beast, whose number is 666, may be traced back to Dan, the Serpent, whose father was the man, Jacob.

- The prophet Amos prophesied that Israel (Jacob) would be laid waste and destroyed:

  "The Lord God hath sworn by himself, saith the Lord the God of hosts, I abhor the excellency of Jacob, and hate his palaces: therefore will I deliver up the city with all that is therein.

  "And it shall come to pass, if there remain ten men in one house, that they shall die...

  "Behold, I will raise up against you a nation, O house of Israel...and they shall afflict you...and the sanctuaries of Israel shall be laid waste." (Amos 6:8-14 and 7:9)

Note in Amos' prophecy that God said, *"I abhor the excellence of Jacob."* God hated the abominations of the fleshly nation of Israel. Jacob had been a spiritual man and beloved of God, but his successors, the wicked physical seed of Israel, God abhorred.

And why shouldn't God hate the "House of Israel?" How obstinate are these people! God has repeatedly warned and punished them for their rebellion and apostasy. But instead of repenting, throughout the centuries they killed the prophets God sent to them, betrayed and murdered Christ, the very Son of God, martyred the angelic Stephen, and persecuted the Apostles.

- And there are the false gods that the rebellious people of Israel worshiped in vain and so offended the true God. What can we make of the deities named *Moloch, Remphan*, and *Chiun*, to whom the six-pointed star served as a symbol of a misplaced devotion?

5 A beast rises up out of the abyss, known also as the bottomless pit (*Revelation 9*)

- ❑ In the Jewish Kabbalah, it is taught that the Messiah and Redeemer ascends from the abyss, or bottomless pit.

- ❑ Also in the Kabbalah, the rabbinical Cohen brothers, from Spain, in their *Treatise on the Left Emanation*, noted the connection between the gematria of "Nachash" (Hebrew for serpent) and the gematria for "Mashiah" (Messiah") is the same and equals 358. The Jews thus say that the words "serpent" and "Messiah" are interconnected.

6 The beast that rises up from the bottomless pit will have a Jewish name.

- ❑ *Revelation 9:11* states that the dark angel who rises up out of the bottomless pit in the last days will have the Hebrew name, Abaddon: "And they had a king over them, which is the angel of the bottomless pit, whose name in the Hebrew tongue is Abaddon, but in the Greek tongue hath his name Apollyon."

In the Kabbalah, the sea beast is called "Leviathan." He is said to be the Messiah and help-mate of the Jewish people. The second beast that comes up out of the earth is a mirror image of the first beast, and is called "Behemoth."

---

7 The beast will suffer a terrible head wound from which he will miraculously recover:

"And he exerciseth all the power of the first beast before him, and causeth the earth and them which dwell therein to worship the first beast, whose deadly wound was healed." (Revelation 13:12)

- ❑ Israel suffered a terrible wound in 70 AD when the Roman General Titus and his army, putting down a rebellion of the Jews, slaughtered hundreds of thousands in Jerusalem and Israel and dispersed many survivors across the known world as slaves and refugees. But, in 1948, the Jews had their nation restored. The beast was, indeed, wounded but was healed.

---

8 The beast will require the inhabitants of earth to take a unique "mark" (or symbol) in their right hand or forehead, which is linked to the number (666) of his name:

"And he causeth all, both small and great, rich and poor, free and bond, to receive a mark in their right hand, or in their foreheads: And that no man might buy or sell, save he that had the mark, or the name of the beast, or the number of his name. Here is wisdom. Let him that hath understanding count the

number of the beast: for it is the number of a man; and his number is six hundred threescore and six."

- ❑ Israel has as its national symbol and on its flag a mark or symbol, the *six-pointed star*, which numerologically translates to the number 666. The star has six points, six triangles, and a hexagram of six lines.

- ❑ *Acts 7:42-43* (and see *Amos 5:25-27*) says that the children of Israel, while in the desert after God miraculously rescued them from the clutches of Pharaoh, betrayed the Lord and began to worship instead the star of their false god:

  "Then God turned, and gave them up to worship the host of heaven (devils)... Yea, ye took up the tabernacle of Moloch, and the star of your god Remphan, figures which ye made to worship them..." (Acts 7:42-43).

In the book of Amos, we find that the children of Israel betrayed the Lord their God and, instead, worshiped the god Moloch. Moloch, the star god, was a god of fire, and the fanatical Israel people literally threw their children into the fire, sacrificing them to Moloch:

"Ye have borne the tabernacle of your Moloch and Chiun your images, the star of your god, which ye made to yourselves. Therefore will I cause you to go into captivity..." (Amos 5:26-27).

- ❑ In the Kabbalah's Tree of Life, the Jews give us the goddess, *Malkuth*. This, in fact, is Moloch. The Jews

The prophet Amos exposed the false god, Moloch, to whom the Israel people sacrificed their own sons and daughters, which caused God to state, *"I abhor the excellency of Jacob...and the sanctuaries of Israel shall be laid waste."*

worship her as "royalty." She is the Creator. She absorbs all the energies of the other gods in her (sexual) regenerative acts. She is the "god of forces" (see *Daniel 11:37-39*) and the embodiment of the nation of Israel. Malkuth, or Moloch, is empowered by the generative energies. Sexual in nature, she is created by the combining of the masculine and feminine. Malkuth is also known for her Serpent Power.

9 The Whore of Babylon, who rides the beast, has the name MYSTERY, BABYLON THE GREAT written on her forehead ("And upon her forehead was a name written, MYSTERY, BABYLON THE GREAT, THE MOTHER OF HARLOTS AND ABOMINATIONS OF THE EARTH") *(Revelation 17:5)*.

Israel was conquered by Nebuchadnezzar, King of Babylon, and spent decades in captivity in Babylon before being released to return to Jerusalem. The Talmud, the Jews most holy book, states that the city of "Babylon" is more sacred to

The World, from the Tarot Card deck of Leisa ReFeo, depicts Malkuth with the global serpent, Oroboros, surrounding her. The Tarot originated in the characters and stories of the Jewish Kabbalah.

God than is Jerusalem. The revealing, formal title of the Talmud is *The Babylonian Talmud.*

---

10 Bible prophecy says that the beast receives his power from the dragon, also known as the serpent, and as Satan, the Devil:

> *"And the great dragon was cast out, that old serpent, called the Devil, and Satan, which deceiveth the whole world: he was cast out into the earth, and his angels were cast out with him" (Revelation 12:9).*

- ❑ The Jewish Kabbalah teaches that the Jewish Messiah is none other than "Leviathan, the Holy Serpent." This is the "beast." Jewish teacher Joel David Bakst, in *"Journey to the Center of the Torah: The Serpent in the Serpent's Belly"* (*chazontorah.org*, 2007), says that the primordial Holy Serpent is "the source of the highest good."

Bakst explains that the Jews are the "serpents inside the serpent."

The Zohar's Book of Concealment, a Kabbalah text, reveals the Holy Serpent to be the "fountainhead, root, and essence for all of God's sacred, revelatory light."

No wonder both John the Baptist and Jesus Christ identified the Jews as a race, or people, of "serpents." Jesus stated: *"Ye serpents, ye generation (race or people) of vipers, how can ye escape the damnation of hell?" (Matthew 23:33).*

---

11 The prophetic vision given to the Apostle John in 95 AD speaks of *"the beast that was, and is not, but shall ascend from out of the bottomless pit" (Revelation 17:8)*.

- ❑ In 95 AD, Israel "was" (i.e. had been), "is not" (had been utterly destroyed a quarter of a century earlier by Titus in 70 AD) "but shall ascend from out of the bottomless pit." In 1948, the latter prophecy was made possible with the reestablishment of the State of Israel.

- ❑ Revelation says that the beast that ascends out of the bottomless pit will have the Hebrew name, "Abaddon" *(Revelation 9:11)*. In the Hebrew language the word Abaddon means "destroyer."

- ❑ The Kabbalah teaches that the Holy Serpent of the Jews "shall ascend out of the bottomless pit" (depicted as the abyss below the center of the kabbalistic Tree of Life) and will empower World Jewry to seize global power and reign over all nations.

- ❑ The words "shall ascend" can be applied to modern-day Israel, a nation that had been destroyed in 70 AD, its people killed or dispersed, and converts made from Khazaria, only to come back ("shall ascend") in 1948 and establish the modern nation of Israel.

12 The Bible says that the antichrist and his people shall be deceitful:

"He shall work deceitfully, for he shall come up and shall become strong with a small people" (Daniel 11:23).

- ❑ The modern-day nation of Israel is well known in political and intelligence networks across the globe as a lying, manipulative, propagandistic world player.

- ❑ The official motto of Israel's secret intelligence service, the Mossad, is *"By Way of Deception."*

---

13 The Antichrist shall enter a rebuilt Temple in Jerusalem and declare that he is "God" and above all other gods:

"Let no man deceive you by any means: for that day shall not come, except there come a falling away first, and that man of sin be revealed, the son of perdition;

"Who opposeth and exalteth himself above all that is called God, or that is worshipped; so that he as God sitteth in the temple of God, shewing himself that he is God (II Thessalonians 2:3-4)."

- ❑ Many Jews and rabbis today have organized and are preparing to rebuild the Temple on the holy mount in Jerusalem. Millions of Jews pray annually at the wailing wall on the Temple Mount in Jerusalem, which they claim is the remains of the old Temple.

---

14 The Antichrist will persecute the saints of God, those who are of Jesus *(Galatians 4:28-31; 5:19-21)* and the Beast will make war against the saints *(Revelation 13:7)*.

- ❏ The New Testament chronicles the horrors inflicted on the Apostles and the early church. Throughout the centuries, Jews are proven to have murdered and vilely treated Christians. Arno Toaff, a Jewish professor at Bar Ilan University in Israel, documented the historical abduction of Gentile children by Jews, their ritual murders, and the drinking of their blood at Passover, in his 2007 book, *Passovers in Blood*.

- ❏ Crypto-Jews known as the Young Turks, staged a coup and took over the Ottoman Empire in Turkey, in 1908. These Jews were responsible for the Armenian Genocide in which one and one-half million Christians were massacred.

Victims of the Armenian Genocide.

Palestinian victims of Israeli massacre

- ❑ In the Soviet Union, Jews Lenin, Trotsky, Yagoda, and others killed 66 million people, mostly Christians, in Gulag concentration camps and other killing arenas.

- ❑ Today, the nation of Israel continues its murderous crimes in their ethnic cleansing of Palestine and their butchery of Lebanon. Their goal is a Greater Israel, which is symbolized by the two horizontal blue lines on the flag of Israel. Their meaning is the Jewish expectation that they will eventually reign from the Euphrates River, which runs next to Baghdad in Iraq, down to the Nile River, in Egypt.

---

15 The Whore of Babylon is fabulously wealthy and is *"decked with gold and precious stones and pearls"* *(Revelation 17:4)*. And the last days King *"shall have power* *over the treasures of gold and of silver" (Daniel 11:43).*

- ❑ Billionaire Jews control the world's gold and precious stones markets and commerce. Across the world it is known that Jewish corporations and merchants run the diamond and precious gems trade. The Oppenheimers and other Jewish families own the world's largest diamond mines in South Africa, Liberia, and elsewhere. The same is true of gold mines. Huge international, Jewish-owned banks Goldman Sachs, JP Morgan Chase, Morgan Stanley, and others control the precious metals and oil futures markets. Goldman Sachs and

Baroness Marie-Helene de Rothschild and Baron Alexis de Rede enjoy themselves at a gala masquerade party in 2011.

Morgan Stanley jointly own the majority of the shares of the International Commodities Exchange (ICE), in London. Lord Rothschild and David Rockefeller recently united their vast banking and oil holdings.

- Although Jews make up only about two percent of America's population, over fifty percent of the billionaires on *Forbes* magazine's annual list of America's richest persons are Jews. That is twenty-five times their proportion of the population. The list of

Jews are at the helm of the world's top high tech corporations, including Facebook, Dell Computers, Hewlett-Packard, Amazon, Oracle Software, Apple Computers, and many more. Here we see Jeff Bezos of Amazon and Bill Gates of Microsoft at a conference.

wealthy Jews includes Apple's Stephen Jobs (now deceased), Microsoft's Bill Gates, Amazon's Jeff Bezos, and Dell's Michael Dell. Of course, the Rothschilds are the most wealthy family on earth, and Jewish dynasties such as the Bronfmans and Reichmans in Canada are not far behind.

❑ That this wealth is more important to the rich Jews than the God of their fathers is made clear in the scriptures. *Daniel 11:37-38* states: "Neither shall he (the last days ruler, or antichrist) regard the God of his fathers… But in his estate shall he honor the god of forces: and a god whom his fathers knew not shall he honor with gold and silver and with precious stones, and pleasant things."

❑ In *I Timothy 6:9-10* we are told that the "love of money is the root of all evil."

❑ In *James 5:1-6* we find this prophecy regarding the global corporate elite (mostly Jews) who enrich themselves in the last days, defraud the working man, and condemn and kill the just who oppose their wickedness.

"Go to now, ye rich men, weep and howl for your miseries that shall come upon you. Your riches are corrupted, and your garments are motheaten. Your gold and silver is cankered; and the rust of them shall be a witness against you, and shall eat your flesh as it were fire. Ye have heaped treasure together for the last days. Behold, the hire of the labourers who have

reaped down your fields, which is of you kept back by fraud, crieth: and the cries of them which have reaped are entered into the ears of the Lord of sabaoth. Ye have lived in pleasure on the earth, and been wanton; ye have nourished your hearts, as in a day of slaughter. Ye have condemned and killed the just; and he doth not resist you." (James 5:1-6)

16 The prophet Daniel says that the last days King (the Antichrist) will not worship the God of his fathers, *"But in his estate shall he honour the God of forces: and a god whom his fathers knew not shall he honour... a strange god..." (Daniel 11:37-39)*

- The reference in the book of Daniel that the Antichrist King would not worship the "God of his fathers" is plainly to the fathers of Israel and the Jews. In *Jeremiah 44:3,* for example, we read: "Because of their wickedness which they have committed to provoke me to anger, in that they went to burn incense, and to serve other gods, whom they knew not, neither they, yea, nor your fathers."

  The fathers of Israel are the patriarchs, Abraham, Moses, Isaac, Jacob, etc., and their God is the great "I Am," the God of the Christians. But the Talmud and the Kabbalah make clear that the Jews do not worship the God of Moses and the prophets, but instead worship a multiplicity of gods and goddesses, all of which the rabbis claim are "aspects," "sparks," or "emanations" from an unknowable, mysterious God called *Ein Sof* (or *Ain Sof*). This "strange god" of the Jews is a god of "forces" and his powers, or force, are derived from cosmic energy produced by the sexual regenerative act. The sexual act results in what is called the "Cosmic Balance."

❑ Contrary to what most Christians erroneously believe, the people of the nation of Israel fought against and killed the prophets and opposed the patriarchs. Jesus sagely noted this when he declared:

"Even so ye also outwardly appear righteous unto men, but within ye are full of hypocrisy and iniquity. Woe unto you, scribes and Pharisees, hypocrites! because ye build the tombs of the prophets, and garnish the sepulchres of the righteous, And say, If we had been in the days of our fathers, we would not have been partakers with them in the blood of the prophets. Wherefore ye be witnesses unto yourselves, that ye are the children of them which killed the prophets. Fill ye up then the measure of your fathers. Ye serpents, ye generation of vipers, how can ye escape the damnation of hell? ... O Jerusalem, Jerusalem, thou that killest the prophets, and stonest them which are sent unto thee, how often would I have gathered thy children together, even as a hen gathereth her chickens under her wings, and ye would not!" (Matthew 23:28-33, 37)

17 The Whore of Babylon rides upon a beast which has seven heads and these seven heads are *"seven mountains" (Revelation 17:9)*. Many prophecy scholars speak of this as "The Great City that sits upon seven hills."

The city of Jerusalem has seven hills, as do the cities of Rome, Istanbul and Moscow. The Temple of the Jews (Solomon's Temple, Herod's Temple) sat upon one of these "mountains."

Jerusalem is the Great City that sits on seven hills *(Revelation 17:9)*.

18 The beautiful and voluptuous Whore of Babylon is full of the *"filthiness of her fornication" (Revelation 17:4)*.

- ❑ The Old Testament prophets described Jerusalem and Israel as a "whore," and as "Babylon," and castigated her for her abominations, fornication and whoredom. For example, in *Ezekiel 16:2* we read: *"Again the word of the Lord came unto me, saying, Son of man, cause Jerusalem to know her abominations...thou didst trust in thine own beauty, and played the harlot... and poured out thine fornications on everyone that passeth by...and did commit whoredom with them...thou hast played the whore... thy filthiness was poured out... and with all the idols of thy abominations..."*

❑ Compare *Revelation 17:4* and the above verses of *Ezekiel 16:2*. Is God not talking about the very same city? "Babylon" is a satanic codeword for Jerusalem!

Also see *Isaiah 47* where *Jerusalem* and its people are called the "daughter of Babylon" and the "daughter of the Chaldean" and is scorned by God for "uncovering the thigh and baring the leg" and doing other "wickedness," including "sorcery" and "enchantments."

19

The woman whose name is written on her forehead or "Mystery, Babylon the Great" is said to be the "Mother of Harlots."

❑ In ancient Babylon, the people worshipped many gods and goddesses and many of the goddesses were "holy prostitutes." The holy sex ritual was practiced in Babylonia's temples. Today's Judaism is rife with sexuality and sexually magnified deities. The Jewish Kabbalah presents multiple gods and goddesses, including the "Supreme Mother," known as "Binah," and her Divine Daughter, Malkuth. Both Binah, the Mother, and the Daughter, Malkuth, have holy sex with a Father God (name "Kether") and a Divine Son (named "Chokmah"). These goddess types also have had sex with Satan whom, the rabbis claim, continually pesters them for more sex. There is also Shekinah, the Divine Presence, a goddess with whom the Jews can and do have virtual sex, or fantasized sex.

- ❑ Judaism is actually a phallic sex cult. Everything evolves around the sex act. The rocking, rythmic motion of the worshiper at the wailing wall in Jerusalem often means that he is engaging in sexual coitus with a god or goddess of the Kabbalah pantheon.

- ❑ Michael Hoffman II, in his scholarly book, *Judaism's Strange Gods*, remarks that, "Judaism is not based on the Old Testament." He adds further that, "Judaism's God is not the God of Israel, but the strange gods and goddesses of the Talmud and Kabbalah."

20 As the "Mother of Harlots" the Whore of Babylon apparently has daughters and has birthed many other whorish religions and cults *(Revelation 17:5)*.

- ❑ History documents that virtually every New Age group and every satanic cult, satanic secret society, and satanic church had and have as their foundation the Kabbalah of the Jews. Freemasonry, Theosophy, the Order of the Golden Dawn, the Church of Satan, Aleister Crowley's Thelema teachings, Mormonism, and countless other groups have their doctrinal origins in the Kabbalah. The Hindu religion and Judaism have many striking parallels, including the concepts of holy sex, many gods and goddesses, idols, talismans, charms, racial castes, reincarnation, karma, and communication with spirits and with the dead.

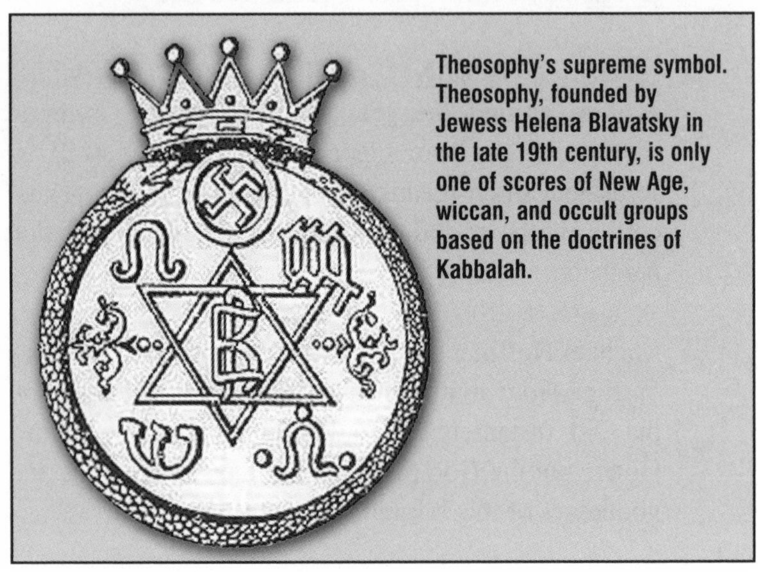

Theosophy's supreme symbol. Theosophy, founded by Jewess Helena Blavatsky in the late 19th century, is only one of scores of New Age, wiccan, and occult groups based on the doctrines of Kabbalah.

21 The Whore, whose name is written as "Mystery, Babylon the Great" "sitteth upon many waters" *(Revelation 17:1)*; and John saw a vision of a beast "rising up out of the sea" *(Revelation 13:1)*.

❑ Dianne Stein, Jewish author of *The Women's Spirituality Book*, writes: "The goddess of all things rose naked from chaos. Separating the sea from the sky, she brooded over the water until she give birth to life: herself." The Kabbalah calls this feminine Deity Leviathan the Serpent, and also Shekinah, and says that she rises out of the chaotic abyss, or bottomless pit and ascends to become Messiah. As Messiah, she becomes one with the Jewish people and teaches them how to collectively and individually become their own Messiah.

- ❑ The references in *Revelation 13:1* to the beast which rises up out of the sea, and in *Revelation 17* to the Harlot, Mystery, Babylon the Great, *"that sitteth upon many waters"* are to the fact, that according to *Revelation 17:1*, this satanic system rules for a time over *"peoples, and multitudes, and nations, and tongues"* (languages):

  > *"And he saith unto me, The waters which thou sawest, where the whore sitteth, are peoples, and multitudes, and nations, and tongues."*

- ❑ We are also told in *Revelation 13:7* that, *"Power was given him (the beast) over all kindreds, and tongues, and nations;"* In *Revelation 13:8* we are told that, *"All that dwell upon the earth shall worship him, whose names are not written in the book of life of the Lamb."* Therefore, the "sea" and "many waters" cited in Revelation refer to the swirling sea or ocean of humanity and to the chaos of humanity.

- ❑ The Jews were dispersed among the nations when General Titus, of Rome, destroyed Jerusalem in 70 AD. Called *The Great Diaspora*, this spreading of the klannish Jews amongst the nations proved a tremendous advantage, allowing the Jewish community in various nations to band together and favor their own kind.

Through racial nepotism, chicanery, and by defrauding the Gentiles whom their Talmud teaches are racial inferiors, the Jews have risen economically in every culture and are dominant in banking, government, education, entertainment and the media. World Jewry does, indeed, rule over "all kindreds, and tongues, and nations." This is why "Aliyah"—the return of the Jews to Israel—has not fully succeeded. The Jews are enjoying success in the countries wherein they reside, but they generally avoid assimilation.

22 John's prophecy of the Four Horsemen of the Apocalypse tells us that the second beast is heard to say, *"Come and see."* John continues: *"And there went out another horse that was red, and power was given him that sat thereon to take peace from the earth, and that they should kill one another: and there was given him a great sword" (Revelation 6:4).*

- The color *red* has tremendous occult and magical significance in Judaic religion and in its Kabbalah. This color is said to bring good luck to its wearer, and many Jews wear a *red-colored* cord bracelet around their wrist. In 1948, the Jewish high council in the fledgling nation of Israel, composed of David Ben-Gurion and other Ashkenazi Jews from Europe, had its headquarters in a building they called the *Red House*. It was here where, according to Jewish historian Ilan Pappe, they mapped out a diabolical plan for the ethnic cleansing of Palestine.

- In Soviet Russia, the *"Reds"* (communists), Lenin, Trotsky, Kaganovich, Zinoviev, and others carried out abominable atrocities. Their purging and murder campaigns were called the *Red Terror*, and Lenin constantly demanded, "more blood." The Soviet flag and military tanks and aircraft wore the symbolic *Red Star*.

- *Revelation 12* symbolically depicts Satan as a "great *red* dragon." It is this dragon that gives the beast that rises up out of the sea (Israel/World Jewry) his *"power, and his seat, and great authority" (Revelation 13:1-2)*.

- The *red* wristband is worn by many followers of Kabbalah, both Jew and Gentile. It has been, for instance, seen on the wrists of Bill and Hillary Clinton, Senator Harry Reid (D-NV), Britney Spears, Madonna, and many other politicians and celebrities.

In sum, *red* is the color of blood and death; *red* (scarlet) is the color worn by the Whore of Babylon; the beast which she rides upon is *red* (scarlet-coloured); the dragon which gives the beast its seat and power is *red*; the greatest Jewish mass murderers of the 20th and 21st centuries have been the *Red* Communists, whose flag is *red* and whose hideous campaign of death and torture is known as the *Red* Terror. Moreover, the Jews who seized power in Palestine, declared Israel a nation, and conducted the horrors of ethnic cleansing against Gentile Palestinian natives called their headquarters in Tel Aviv, the "*Red* House."

23 "Mystery, Babylon the Great" is described as a sensuous and beautiful woman, a whore *(Revelation 17)*, She is linked in Bible prophecy with the beast whose number is 666 *(Revelation 13:18)*.

- ❑ Barbara Walker, author of the *Women's Encyclopedia of Myths and Secrets*, remarks that, "The Miraculous Number 666 was very, very holy in the Egyptian religion of the Goddess." Walker states of the Goddess: "Babylonian 'star,' the Great Goddess, who appears in the Bible as Ashtoreth, Anath, Asherah...the Queen of Heaven. She was also the Great Whore, described in *Revelation 17:5* as 'Babylon the Great, the Mother of Harlots...' Men communed with her through the sexual rites of her harlot princesses."

- ❑ The prophet Jeremiah also linked the nation of Israel to the worship of the Great Goddess, the Babylonian "Queen of Heaven:"

> *"Seest thou not what they do in the cities of Judah and in the streets of Jerusalem? ...the women knead their dough, to make cakes to the queen of heaven, and to pour out drink offerings unto other gods, that they may provoke me to anger" (Jeremiah 7:17-18).*

- ❑ Just as the occult number 666 was very holy in the Egyptian and Babylonian religions of the Goddess, so also the number of the beast and name of the antichrist, 666, has special significance in Judaism as a positive, good, and holy number. In the Kabbalah's Zohar, we are told that to the Jews the number 666 conceals *"exalted and lofty messianic potential."* In addition, the number 666, in Judaism, is said to represent *"the strength and perfection of the physical world"* which will be realized in the coming messianic age of the Jewish Kingdom on earth (see online Jewish education website, *ohr.edu/sixsixsix*).

---

24 Mystery, Babylon the Great is to rule over the last days great world empire, but that empire shall become *"the habitation of devils, and the hold of every foul spirit, and a cage of every unclean bird" (Revelation 18:1-2).*

- At the foundation of the Judaic religion are the many books of the Kabbalah. These teachings are the very fabric woven into the many rituals, practices, and doctrines of the Jewish religion and spiritual life. But these teachings are blatantly occultic and darkly satanic. Many rabbis admit that the Kabbalah is the father of most of the world's occult societies, orders, cults, and sects. Albert Pike, former Sovereign Grand Commander of Scottish Rite Freemasonry, admitted in his textbook, *Morals and Dogma*, that the rituals of Freemasonry in all its degrees come from the Kabbalah. Both Aleister Crowley, the infamous British occultist, and Anton Szander LaVey, founder of America's 20th century Church of Satan, borrowed from the Kabbalah. So did their wicked 19th century predecessors, Helena Blavatsky, founder of Theosophy, and Eliphas Levi, Satanist of France.

- The New Age movement of the late 20th century,

Aleister Crowley (top, left), the 20th Century's infamous British satanist, Anton LaVey, (top, right) founder of America's Church of Satan, and Albert Pike, 19th Century Sovereign Grand Commander of Scottish Rite Freemasonry, all gave credit to the Jewish Kabbalah for the rituals, ceremonies, and teachings of their respective occult organizations.

whose false prophets and teachers continue to prosper, was birthed by kabbalistic Jews. Many of the most popular New Age gurus and spiritualists were Jewish men and women who adopted new names to hide their Jewish identity. Jack Rosenberg became Werner Erhard of EST, Richard Alpert took on the name Ram Dass, etc. The popular New Age book, *A Course in Miracles,* was authored by Helen Schucman, a Jewish psychologist.

❑ As if this weren't enough, it has been demonstrated that it was the Jews, Karl Marx, Vladimir Lenin, and Leon Trotsky, who brought into the world the horrors and barbarism of Bolshevism and Communism. The bloodlust atrocities of the Spanish Inquisition (led by Torquemada, a Jew), and the destruction and carnage of the French Revolution, with the Jew, Adam Weishaupt, as founder of the Illuminati being the ideological mastermind, and the Jew, Robespierre, the major executioner by guillotine of the innocent.

Truly, it can be said that revolutionary World Jewry has proven in every way feasible to be the font of world violence and is become, *"the habitat of devils, and the hold of every foul spirit, and a cage of every unclean bird."*

---

25 The Scriptures prophesy that Mystery Babylon will fall *twice*:

"And he cried mightily with a strong voice, saying, 'Babylon the Great is fallen, is fallen...'" (Rev 18:1-2).

Then again, in *Revelation 14:8*, we are told:

> *"And there followed another angel, saying, Babylon is fallen, is fallen, that great city, because she made all nations drink of the wine of the wrath of her fornication."*

❑ The ancient city of Babylon, in southern Iraq, is now in ruins, but Bible prophecy speaks not of her but of Israel as Mystery Babylon.

❑ Israel had a great fall in 70 AD when the Roman General Titus invaded, destroyed the Temple and the city of Jerusalem, slew many thousands of its inhabitants, and dispersed the surviving population. This was fall number one and the "desolation" thereof continued until the year 1948. But, the Scriptures prophesy a second coming, greater and final, fall of "Babylon" (codeword for Israel) and she *"shall be utterly burned with fire" (Revelation 18:8).*

❑ It is interesting to note that on Rothschild Boulevard in the Israeli city of Tel Aviv, founded by Lord Rothschild in 1909, there is a plaque mounted on a prominent, now historic home so that all who pass by may read it. The words are in regard to the rise of fallen Israel: *"Again I will rebuild thee and thou shalt be rebuilt."*

26 In *Matthew 23:34-35* Jesus directly identified and accused the House of Israel (the Jews) of being guilty and responsible for all the righteous blood ever shed on planet earth.

"Wherefore, behold, I send unto you prophets, and wise men, and scribes: and some of them ye shall kill and crucify; and some of them shall ye scourge in your synagogues, and persecute them from city to city: That upon you may come all the righteous blood shed upon the earth, from the blood of righteous Abel unto the blood of Zacharias son of Barachias, whom ye slew between the temple and the altar."

Compare the above verse, in *Matthew*, with this prophetic verse in *Revelation 18* which refers to Mystery, Babylon the Great:

"And in her was found the blood of prophets, and of saints, and of all that were slain upon the earth." (Revelation 18:24)

---

27 When the Pharisees demanded of Jesus a sign, he rebuked them and said unto them:

"When the unclean spirit is gone out of a man, he walketh through dry places, seeking rest, and findeth none."

"Then he saith, I will return into my house from whence I came out; and when he is come, he findeth it empty, swept, and garnished."

"Then goeth he, and taketh with himself seven other spirits more wicked than himself, and they enter in and dwell there: and the last state of that man is worse than the first. Even so shall it be also unto this wicked generation."

So, in all, there are *eight* unclean spirits mentioned by Christ. Finding the house empty, swept, and garnished, the first will return, bringing with him seven more.

According to *Webster's Dictionary* and *Strong's Concordance*, the word "generation" means race, ethnic group, nation, or house (as in the "House of Israel"). Israel had swept and garnished its house, but it was left "empty," and so, *seven* other spirits entered therein. And the last day state of physical Israel (World Jewry) is worse than the first.

In *Revelation 17* we find a similar parallel. The Whore, Mystery, Babylon the Great, sits upon a beast "having seven heads and ten horns." In addition to these "seven heads" are "seven kings" who will lead the nation of Israel. Each of the seven will be possessed by a devil, or unclean spirit. Thus, there will be "seven unclean spirits" come in to the House of Israel, and they will be subsequently joined by an eighth such unclean spirit:

"And there are seven kings...and the beast that was, and is not, even he is the eighth and of the seven, and goeth into perdition" (Revelation 17:10-11).

28 The last days King (the antichrist) will come to power even though his people, or nation, will be small:

> *"...he shall work deceitfully: for he shall come up, and shall become strong with a small people" (Daniel 11:23).*

In the whole world, demographers say there are at most nineteen million Jews (out of a global population of seven billion). The tiny nation of Israel has a population of 7.5 million. So World Jewry, relative to other races, peoples, and nations, is indeed quite "small," and yet, because of the Jews' combined wealth and its political and military power vested in such powerhouse proxy nations as the United States, Great Britain, and France, the 21st century House of Israel (World Jewry) is a strong power. Without even considering its external allies, military experts rate Israel as possessing the world's sixth greatest military force. It is one of a handful of nations which has nuclear bombs and the means (missiles and submarines) to launch them.

---

29 The last days King will be deceptive and use *craft* (black magic, occultism, and sorcery) against his enemies.

We have seen that this latter days leader and his people *"shall work deceitfully" (Daniel 11:23). Daniel 11:24* says also that *"he shall forecast his (occult) devices against the strongholds."*

- ❑ The Kabbalah of the Jews is the basis of much of the world's black magic and occultism. Every dark method is included, from necromancy to sex with devils.

- ❑ The Talmud is also infested with recommendations for

and descriptions of satanic occult powers, including snake charming and demon seduction and magic.

30 The last days "King" will win his kingdom and acquire great power by cleverly employing *"flattery:"*

"And in his estate shall stand up a vile person, to whom they shall not give the honour of the kingdom: but he shall come in peaceably, and obtain the kingdom by flattery" (Daniel 11:21).

- ❑ As is true of every person and race, the Jews are easily seduced by "flattery," and this will be their downfall, for the Antichrist will be a cunning leader who shall win recognition as Messiah and King by flattery. The Talmud flatters by declaring Jews to be a divine race, a holy bloodline, racially superior to the Gentiles, who are said to be goyim (cattle, animals, beast).

- ❑ The Kabbalah and Talmud teach that the Messiah will move to utterly destroy all Gentiles who refuse to worship the Jews. This is called the "Day of Purification" by rabbis.

- ❑ The Jews will become "gods." What greater flattery than to be praised and held up as gods on earth.

31 The beast and antichrist will speak great *blasphemies:*

"And there was given unto him (the first beast, who rises up out of the sea) a mouth speaking great things and blasphemies... And he opened his mouth in blasphemy against God, to blaspheme his name, and his tabernacle, and them that dwell in heaven" (Revelation 13:5).

- Surely, no other people or religion on earth has blasphemed God, his name, his tabernacle, the heavenly host, and the saints of the Most High as much as the Jews. In the Talmud, the sacred book containing their *Halakhah* (613 laws and commentary), the Jewish sages, the most respected of the rabbis throughout history, Jesus Christ is branded a "bastard" and a "fornicator with animals." The Talmud claims Jesus was a "black magician" who used sex magick and talismans. The Talmud also calls Jesus' Mother, Mary, a whore and alleges she had sex with many men and that her sexual relationship with a Roman centurion produced her illegitimate offspring, Jesus. Of course, no evidence is presented for these blasphemous allegations.

  According to the Talmud, Jesus is being punished today for his many sins and abominable acts and for his betrayal of Israel by being boiled in a huge vat of hot, fiery excrement. What greater *blasphemy* can there be than this?

- Blasphemy towards Christians is also in great evidence. As to the Christian saints, the Talmud teaches that faithful Christians shall have no part in the future world. It instructs the Jews to kill Christians whenever possible (when they can get away with it), to spit three times on the ground and utter a curse when they pass by a Christian church, to ritually spit on the graves of Christians, to freely cheat and defraud Christians in business deals, and so on. Christians are said to be immoral, evil, and not to be trusted. They are deemed the Goyim, which means, cattle.

According to the *Hatanya*, a fundamental Judaic book that is a continuous bestseller, all non-Jews are totally satanic creatures in whom there is absolutely nothing good. The very existence of non-Jews is *"inessential,"* whereas, *"all of creation was created solely for the Jews."*

- The host of heaven is blasphemed in Judaism. For example, the names of infernal angels (Metatron, Azazel, etc.) are often called upon by Jews, and the Jews claim there are many strange spirit entities which inhabit heaven. The Kabbalah of the Jews posits the satanic belief that the great "God" is none other than an impersonal and unknowable being called "Ain Sof." From Ain Sof are emitted sparks of light, one of which is "Leviathan the Holy Serpent." In the Jews' Tree of Life, we find the names of other deities and manifestations of the Divine, all of which masquerade as "emanations" or "aspects" of the one God. They often are worshipped individually as gods. The names of these gods and goddesses of Judaism include Binah, Chokmah, Malkuth, Hesod, and others. This is absolutely blasphemy for it attributes His glory and majesty to demon gods and false gods and goddesses.

❑ In no other religion—no, not in Hinduism, Islam, Buddhism, Taoism, or any other sect—can one find such abject blasphemy, thus proving that World Jewry actively encourages vile hatred and blasphemy against God, the Son of God, his name, and them that dwell in heaven, and the saints. *The Jews are the Blasphemers of all Blasphemers!*

---

32 Their Father is the Devil. The most wicked religious system on earth is the one whose leaders and followers have Satan as their Father. They are the ones who shall make war against the saints, and persecute and kill many *(Revelation 13)*.

"I know thy works, and tribulation, and poverty, (but thou art rich) and I know the blasphemy of them which say they are Jews, and are not, but are the synagogue of Satan" (Revelation 2:9).

"Behold, I will make them of the synagogue of Satan, which say they are Jews, and are not, but do lie; behold, I will make them to come and worship before thy feet, and to know that I have loved thee" (Revelation 3:9).

❑ In *John 8:39-47*, Jesus Christ bluntly told the Jews that Satan, not God, is their Father:

"If God were your Father, ye would love me: for I proceeded forth and came from God; neither came I of myself, but he sent me. Why do ye not

understand my speech? even because ye cannot hear my word. Ye are of your father the devil, and the lusts of your father ye will do..." (John 8:42-44)

❑ Israeli scholar Israel Shahak, in his excellent book, *Jewish History, Jewish Religion: The Weight of Three Thousand Years*, reports Jews today worship both God and Satan. The Jews often pray to Satan and seek his counsel and help. "The kabbalists," says Shahak, "believe that some of the sacrifices burnt in the (ancient) Temple were intended for Satan."

"Many Jews," Shahak writes, "performing a given religious ritual, believe it to be an act of worship toward God, while others do exactly the same thing with the intention of propitiating Satan."

❑ Harold Rosenthal, former top aide to U.S. Senator Jacob Javits (R-NY), in the 1976 book, *Hidden Tyranny*, confessed that Jews do actually worship Satan, or Lucifer: "Our god is Lucifer…we are his chosen people."

33 Those whose Father is the Devil have a specific religious system to which they belong. It is called the "Synagogue of Satan" *(Revelation 2:9; 3:9)*.

❑ God's prophetic Word, in *Revelation 2:9* and *3:9*, specifically names the *"Synagogue of Satan"* as the wicked, last days religious system. Take note that the Scriptures do not mention the Moslems, or the

Buddhists, the Hindus, the Roman Catholic Church, or any other group. God wants His people expressly to know that it is the Synagogue of Satan that shall bring to pass the horrific events of Revelation. The Moslems have mosques, the Hindus have temples and ashrams, but it is the *Synagogue of Satan* which Christians are warned to watch and beware. The Jews' Synagogue of Satan is the source and font of endtime evil; and it is the designated House of Satan.

❑ In fact, it is only the Jews whose sacred books of the Talmud and the Kabbalah are filled with such terrible hate and vituperation toward Jesus and His Christian disciples. Neither the Hindu *Bhagavad Gita* nor Islam's *Koran* call Jesus a "bastard," a "fornicator," and worse. Only the Jews' religion does this, and only the synagogues teach that one race—the Jews—is superior and divine and that all others are made up of the goyim (inferior animals, or cattle).

---

34 According to the book of Revelation, the Synagogue of Satan will persecute the Christian saints, have some thrown in prison, and put many to death:

> *"And unto the angel of the church in Smyrna write; These things saith the first and the last, which was dead, and is alive; I know thy works, and tribulation, and poverty, (but thou art rich) and I know the blasphemy of them which say they are Jews, and are not, but are the synagogue of Satan. Fear none of those things which thou shalt suffer:*

behold, the devil shall cast some of you into prison, that ye may be tried; and ye shall have tribulation ten days: be thou faithful unto death, and I will give thee a crown of life. He that hath an ear, let him hear what the Spirit saith unto the churches; He that overcometh shall not be hurt of the second death" (Revelation 2:8-11).

❑ The Talmud advises: "The best of the gentiles—kill!"

❑ Ever since Jesus was crucified at the insistence of the Jews, the rabbis and Jewish leaders have sought to kill Christians and extinguish the light of Christian truth. The book of Acts in the New Testament chronicles the hatred of the Jews toward the followers of Jesus. The Apostles found themselves harassed, beaten, thrown into prison, and many were murdered, all at the behest of the Jews. The Jews spread lies and false rumors about Christians and tried to persuade Caesar and his Roman officials that the Christians were traitors and wanted to dethrone the Roman Emperor. *Foxe's Book of Martyrs* and many other reference books document the fatal campaigns of the Jews and the suffering of Christians under the assault of the Synagogue of Satan.

❑ Throughout the centuries, Jews in positions of power in Church and State have targeted Christians for persecution and death. The Spanish Inquisition in which hundreds of thousands were so cruelly tortured and killed was led by a Spanish Jew Marrano (convert). The Communist era, in which tens of millions of Christians perished, was fostered by Jews Marx, Lenin,

Trotsky, and Kaganovich.

- To this day, Jewish organizations and Jewish founded organizations—the Anti-Defamation League (ADL), ACLU, World Jewish Congress, American Jewish Congress, Southern Poverty Law Center, the American Israel Public Affairs Committee (AIPAC), and others—are doing their utmost, I believe, to persecute Christians and wipe out every vestige of Christianity from American culture.

- Jewish producers and directors in Hollywood and on Broadway continually produce movies and TV productions and Broadway plays that mock and denigrate Christians and the Lord Jesus. The media, including the book industry, owned and ran primarily by Jews, discriminates against and targets Christian values and the Christian church for ridicule and mockery.

- The Jews have caused governments in Canada, Sweden, Germany, France, Austria, Great Britain, Australia, and around the world to pass "Hate Crime" Laws making it a punishable offense to criticize Jews or Israel or to question whether the tainted "official history" of World War II and the holocaust is accurate. In Australia, a man was recently indicted and found guilty of debating a Zionist Jew and saying that the religion of Judaism is "Satanic." Hundreds have been incarcerated and now sit in prison cells simply for expressing their opinions or for openly stating the provable facts on such matters.

- The Jewish lobby and interests are so powerful and so vehement in their hatred of Christianity and the truth that although western nations have Constitutions and Charters that protect free speech, these are over-ridden so that the Jews can shield their lies and their false history from public scrutiny.

---

35 The prophetic scriptures speak of a *"great city"* where the rebuilt Temple of God is located and in which the two witnesses of God will prophesy for "a thousand two hundred and threescore days." After they have finished their testimony, *"The beast that ascendeth out of the bottomless pit shall make war against them, and shall overcome them, and kill them" (Revelation 11:1-9).*

- In *Revelation 11:8*, we find proof that this great city where the beast ascends out of the bottomless pit and kills the two witnesses of God is none other than Jerusalem, where Jesus was tried and crucified at Calvary. Jerusalem is prophesied to be so wicked and evil in the last days it is spiritually called "Sodom and Egypt:"

  "And their (the two witnesses) dead bodies shall lie in the street of the great city...where also our Lord was crucified" (Revelation 11:8).

---

36 In the last days, those who make themselves the enemies of God and the enemies of the Lamb of God

(Jesus) and who have the mark (six-pointed star) of the beast and worship the image of the beast (the restored, latter days nation of Israel) shall suffer the wrath of God:

> *"And I heard a great voice out of the temple saying to the seven angels, Go your ways, and pour out the vials of the wrath of God upon the earth. And the first went, and poured out his vial upon the earth; and there fell a noisome and grievous sore upon the men which had the mark of the beast, and upon them which worshipped his image. And the second angel poured out his vial upon the sea; and it became as the blood of a dead man: and every living soul died in the sea. And the third angel poured out his vial upon the rivers and fountains of waters; and they became blood" (Revelation 16:1-4).*

> *"And the fourth angel poured out his vial upon the sun; and power was given unto him to scorch men with fire. And men were scorched with great heat, and blasphemed the name of God, which hath power over these plagues: and they repented not to give him glory. And the fifth angel poured out his vial upon the seat of the beast; and his kingdom was full of darkness; and they gnawed their tongues for pain, And blasphemed the God of heaven because of their pains and their sores, and repented not of their deeds" (Revelation 16:8-11).*

❑ Throughout the centuries, the Jews have made themselves the enemies of the nations in which they have sojourned and been dispersed. Their stubbornness, pride, contrary nature, their evil works, grievous crimes, treacherous dealings, and hatred of all but their own kind have earned them the enmity of all nations and peoples. The Jews, of course, attempt to dodge their own heavy responsibility by crying, "anti-Semitism."

It is true that in past eras, Jews have often been persecuted. Because of their hatred and lack of respect for Gentiles, Jews have been the victims of pogroms in many nations, especially in the Middle East, in 19th century Russia, and in Germany during the Nazi era. Although the suffering of the Jews during the legendary Holocaust is greatly exaggerated, it is a fact that the Nazis passed laws confiscating the property of Jews, restricting their movement, and limiting their occupational choices. Finally, many Jews wherever the armed forces of Germany gained control—in Poland, Russia, Hungary, Czechoslovakia, and other occupied nations—were rounded up and placed in labor camps where living conditions were harsh. In the last months of World War II, the bombing of the allied air forces (the British and the U.S.) caused untold tragedy for all of Europe and Germany. Food became scarce; energy supplies to stave off the bitter cold were scarce, and no-one, anywhere had medicines and medical supplies. Diseases such as typhoid, influenza, and pneumonia ravaged the labor camp populations.

❑ According to Bible prophecies, the past suffering of the Jews during the Nazi era and in previous epochs are the consequences of their continuing rebellion against God, His Son, Jesus, and the host of heaven, and the saints (Christians) of the Most High.

Unfortunately, because the Jews scorn repentance and even magnify their blasphemies, the House of Israel will suffer greater tragedies in days to come.

"The seat of the beast (Jerusalem); and his kingdom was full of darkness; and they gnawed their tongues for pain, And blasphemed the God of heaven because of their pains and their sores, and repented not of their deeds" (Revelation 16:10-11).

---

37 The Whore of Babylon and the scarlet-colored beast upon which she rides is consumed with hatred for God and His remnant on earth and will go forth to kill and conquer, and shall make war against the saints:

"And I saw the woman drunken with the blood of the saints, and with the blood of the martyrs of Jesus" (Revelation 17:6).

- For this reason—their abominable crimes committed against God's people on earth, the saints and martyrs of Jesus, those who had the mark of the beast and them who worshipped his image and blasphemed, have poured out on them *"the vials of the wrath of God" (Revelation 16:1)*:

  "For they have shed the blood of saints and prophets" (Revelation 16:6).

- Again we recall that Jesus prophesied of God's

judgment on these grievous sins of the House of Israel:

"Woe unto you, scribes and Pharisees, hypocrites! because ye build the tombs of the prophets, and garnish the sepulchres of the righteous, And say, If we had been in the days of our fathers, we would not have been partakers with them in the blood of the prophets. Wherefore ye be witnesses unto yourselves, that ye are the children of them which killed the prophets. Fill ye up then the measure of your fathers.

"Ye serpents, ye generation of vipers, how can ye escape the damnation of hell? Wherefore, behold, I send unto you prophets, and wise men, and scribes: and some of them ye shall kill and crucify; and some of them shall ye scourge in your synagogues, and persecute them from city to city: That upon you may come all the righteous blood shed upon the earth, from the blood of righteous Abel unto the blood of Zacharias son of Barachias, whom ye slew between the temple and the altar" (Matthew 23:29-35).

It is, then, God's judgment that the House of Israel (World Jewry, including the latter day nation of Israel) suffer the pangs and pain to be inflicted on the earth by the pouring out of the vials of God's wrath, for they, and they alone, are adjudged guilty of *"all the righteous blood shed upon the earth, from the blood of righteous*

Abel unto the blood of Zacharias..." (Matthew 23:35).

❑ This judgment of the unrepentant Jews by God, revealing their tragic end, is also repeated and confirmed in *Revelation 18:9: 20, 24*, where God's Word, referring to Babylon the Great, states:

"Therefore shall her plagues come in one day, death, and mourning, and famine; and she shall be utterly burned with fire: for strong is the Lord God who judgeth her...

"Rejoice over her, thou heaven, and ye holy apostles and prophets; for God hath avenged you on her...

"And in her was found the blood of prophets, and of saints, and of all that were slain upon the earth"

---

38 The Bible prophesies that "Babylon the Great" will become a tremendously rich global trading colossus:

"For all nations have drunk of the wine of the wrath of her fornication, and the kings of the earth have committed fornication with her, and the merchants of the earth are waxed rich through the abundance of her delicacies...

"And the kings of the earth, who have committed fornication and lived deliciously with her, shall bewail her, and lament for her, when they shall see the smoke of her burning, Standing afar off for the fear of her torment, saying, Alas, alas, that great city Babylon, that mighty city! for in one hour is thy judgment come.

"And the merchants of the earth shall weep and mourn over her; for no man buyeth their merchandise any more: The merchandise of gold, and silver, and precious stones, and of pearls, and fine linen, and purple, and silk, and scarlet, and all thyine wood, and all manner vessels of ivory, and all manner vessels of most precious wood, and of brass, and iron, and marble,

"And cinnamon, and odours, and ointments, and frankincense, and wine, and oil, and fine flour, and wheat, and beasts, and sheep, and horses, and chariots, and slaves, and souls of men.

"And the fruits that thy soul lusted after are departed from thee, and all things which were dainty and goodly are departed from thee, and thou shalt find them no more at all.

"The merchants of these things, which were made rich by her, shall stand afar off for the fear of her torment, weeping and wailing, And saying, Alas, alas, that great city, that was clothed in fine linen, and purple, and scarlet, and decked with gold, and precious stones, and pearls! For in one hour so

great riches is come to nought. And every shipmaster, and all the company in ships, and sailors, and as many as trade by sea, stood afar off, And cried when they saw the smoke of her burning, saying, What city is like unto this great city!

"And they cast dust on their heads, and cried, weeping and wailing, saying, Alas, alas, that great city, wherein were made rich all that had ships in the sea by reason of her costliness! for in one hour is she made desolate" (Revelation 18:3, 9-19).

- To accomplish their global commercial activities, Jews are concentrated in rich trading nations like the United States, Great Britain, Germany, France, Italy, etc.

- World Jewry has become the reserve of the wealthiest men on this planet. *Forbes*, the premier financial publication, recently published its *Forbes 100*, a list of America's 100 richest men. Fifty-one of the 100 were Jews, even though only two percent of the overall population is Jewish. Jewish billionaires own the world's largest banks and investment houses—JP Morgan Chase, Bank of America, Goldman Sachs, Morgan Stanley, Barclays, UBS, and others. They own majority interest in the lion's share of the world's high tech corporations (Microsoft, Dell Computers, Oracle Software, Amazon, Facebook, Yahoo, Hewlett-Packard). For half a century, the chairman of the Federal Reserve Board has been a Jew. The heads of the Securities and Exchange Commission (SEC), Federal Deposit Insurance Corporation (FDIC), and the Commodities Futures Trading Commission, are all

Jews, as are the heads of the top stock and commodities exchanges on Wall Street, and in London, Paris, Rome, and Chicago. That includes the gigantic New York Stock Exchange and NASDQ in the U.S. and the International Commodity Exchange (ICE) in London.

The Jews' Money Power gives World Jewry control of the world's greatest economic powerhouses in North America and Europe. Jewish interests are extensive in Russia, Africa, South America, the Middle East, and in Asia.

- ❑ The huge oil companies are owned by Jews—Rothschild controls BP and Shell, for example. The Rothschild family is the most wealthy on earth.

- ❑ The gold, silver, and precious stones markets are all controlled by Jews—for example, the DeBeers and Oppenheimer families run the world diamond markets.

- ❑ Men and women with Jewish names like Silverstein, Rothstein, Goldman, Copperstone, Lauder and Feinberg have their names on the most valuable of real estate and they run the lucrative real estate markets.

- ❑ World Jewry, indisputably, is commercial Babylon the Great.

39 There are many evidences in the Bible that Jerusalem and Israel are "Mystery Babylon." The Apostle Peter wrote an epistle (*The First Epistle of Peter*) addressed to

Christians who are the elect, saved by Jesus, scattered throughout "Pontus, Galatia, Cappadocia, Asia, and Bithynia" in which his closing stated: *"The church that is at Babylon, elected together with you, saluteth you; and so doth Marcus my son" (I Peter 5:13).*

- ❑ Church history documents that Peter was the head of the church and believers in Jerusalem, and not in Babylon. Yet, in *I Peter 5:13* (see above), Peter labeled Jerusalem, *"the church that is at Babylon."* At the time this Epistle was written, the ancient city of Babylon lay in ruins and had no inhabitants. The saints and elect of Christ called "Jerusalem" by the codeword, "Babylon," for it was the center and font of the hatred spewed out on Christians throughout the Roman Empire. Wherever Christians suffered from Roman oppression and terror, it was caused by the hatred and animosity of the Jews who had local agents and zealots in all the Roman provinces. Thus, Jerusalem was viewed by early Christians as wicked "Babylon" and its actions in opposition to the Church were couched in terms like "Babylon" to protect the speaker.

40 The Scriptures clearly tell us that he who denies Jesus is the Christ is "antichrist:"

"Who is a liar but he that denieth that Jesus is the Christ? He is antichrist, that denieth the Father and the Son. Whosoever denieth the Son, the same hath not the Father: (but) he that acknowledgeth the Son hath the Father also" (1 John 2:22-23).

❑ Of all the world's religions, it is Judaism that most vehemently denies that Jesus is the Christ. The Talmud expressly says that Jesus is not the Son of God but rather is a liar and a blasphemer who today deservedly is in hell.

In so doing, the Jews make themselves into antichrist and bring upon themselves the judgment and sentence that, "Whosoever denieth the Son hath not the Father."

This confirms Jesus' statement to the Jews: *"Ye are of your father the devil"* (John 8:44).

---

41 The Scriptures say that the earthly city of Jerusalem and her children, the Jews, are in bondage to Satan:

> *"For it is written, that Abraham had two sons, the one by a bondmaid, the other by a freewoman. But he who was of the bondwoman was born after the flesh; but he of the freewoman was by promise.*
>
> *"Which things are an allegory: for these are the two covenants; the one from the mount Sinai, which gendereth to bondage, which is Agar. For this Agar is mount Sinai in Arabia, and answereth to Jerusalem which now is, and is in bondage with her children. But Jerusalem which is above is free, which is the mother of us all.*
>
> *"For it is written, Rejoice, thou barren that bearest not; break forth and cry, thou that travailest not: for*

the desolate hath many more children than she which hath an husband.

"Now we, brethren, as Isaac was, are the children of promise. But as then he that was born after the flesh persecuted him that was born after the Spirit, even so it is now.

"Nevertheless what saith the scripture? Cast out the bondwoman and her son: for the son of the bondwoman shall not be heir with the son of the freewoman. So then, brethren, we are not children of the bondwoman, but of the free" (Galatians 4:22-31).

"Stand fast therefore in the liberty wherewith Christ hath made us free, and be not entangled again with the yoke of bondage" (Galatians 5:1).

❑ In these key verses in *Galatians*, Paul explains that there are *two* Jerusalems. One is earthly or physical Jerusalem, which is of the Jews, and this Jerusalem is allegorically Agar (or Hagar), the slave who bore a son, Ishmael, to Abraham. Thus, earthly Jerusalem, made up of the Jews, is in slavery. To whom are the Jews in bondage and slavery? The answer is: Satan, for men belong either to Satan or to God. So earthly Jerusalem and the Jews are of Satan.

But Jerusalem which is above (that is, the New Jerusalem, or heavenly Jerusalem) is free. Her children are the spiritual descendants of Sarah, the freewoman, who also bore a son to Abraham. The name of that son was Isaac. Now Isaac was born after the promise, and

Christians (the "brethren") are also of the promise. They are born in Christ Jesus and are citizens of the heavenly Jerusalem.

- ❑ Paul makes clear in *Galatians* that the children born of the *Spirit*, that is, after the *promise* (Christians) are *persecuted* by those born after the *flesh* (Jews).

42 The Scriptures say that the Jews, being born after the flesh and having Agar (or Hagar) as their Mother, are in bondage to the Devil. As such, they persecute Christians, who being born of the Spirit, are of the freewoman, Sarah, and are free.

The Scriptures also say that the bondwoman and her son (the Jews) shall be "cast out" and "shall not be heir" to the Kingdom of God, which is the promise:

> *"Now we, brethren, as Isaac was, are the children of promise. But as then he that was born after the flesh persecuted him that was born after the Spirit, even so it is now. Nevertheless what saith the scripture? Cast out the bondwoman and her son: for the son of the bondwoman shall not be heir with the son of the freewoman. So then, brethren, we are not children of the bondwoman, but of the free" (Galatians 3:28-31).*

- ❑ The unmistakable import of this prophecy is that the fleshly children of Israel, the Jews, are not heirs to the Kingdom. The promise is given only to the spiritual children of God, who believe in Jesus and have been set free by His shed blood. The Jews will not receive the Kingdom (i.e. the Promise) but instead, will be cast out for they shall not be heir.

Thus shall be fulfilled the prophecies of Jesus who preached:

"And I say unto you, That many shall come from the east and west, and shall sit down with Abraham, and Isaac, and Jacob, in the kingdom of heaven. But the children of the kingdom shall be cast out into outer darkness: there shall be weeping and gnashing of teeth" (Matthew 8:11-12).

Jesus reiterated this warning to the Jews in *Luke 14:28-30:*

"For which of you, intending to build a tower, sitteth not down first, and counteth the cost, whether he have sufficient to finish it? Lest haply, after he hath laid the foundation, and is not able to finish it, all that behold it begin to mock him, Saying, This man began to build, and was not able to finish."

---

43 Neither the beast, nor the false prophet shall have a part in the Kingdom of God. Instead, they shall be cast into the lake of fire:

"And the devil that deceived them was cast into the lake of fire and brimstone, where the beast and the

false prophet are, and shall be tormented day and night for ever and ever" (Revelation 20:10).

- ❑ We read in *Galatians 4* that the children of Israel after the flesh, in bondage to Satan, shall be "cast out" of the Kingdom. In *Matthew 21* Jesus spoke of this in his parable of the "householder" (owner) of the vineyard who rented (let) out his vineyard to husbandmen (tenant farmers) and went into a far country. When the time of the harvest was near, the householder sent his servants to the husbandmen so that they might receive the fruits of it. But the husbandmen beat one, stoned a second, and killed another of his servants.

  So the householder sent other servants and the evil and greedy husbandmen did likewise to them.

  Finally, the householder sent his son reckoning that, surely, they would reverence his son.

  But when the husbandmen saw the son they conspired and said among themselves, *"This is the heir; come, let us kill him, and let us seize on his inheritance."*

  And so they caught the householder's son, cast him out of the vineyard, and murdered him.

  Jesus then asked of the Jews, *"When the Lord therefore of the vineyard cometh, what will he do unto those husbandmen?"*

  The Jews answered Jesus, and said unto him, *"He will miserably destroy those wicked men, and will let out* (rent) *unto other husbandmen, which shall render him the fruits in their seasons."*

  The Jews apparently had no idea that Jesus was speaking of them and prophesying what they would soon do to Him. Jesus indeed was the Son and Heir,

His Father was the Lord and householder and the Jews were the wicked husbandmen who repeatedly beat and killed the Lord's servants and, finally, slew the Son.

- ❑ Jesus was in fact, prophesying that they would murder him, and seize the Kingdom for themselves. And so...

"Jesus saith unto them, Did ye never read in the scriptures, The stone which the builders rejected, the same is become the head of the corner: this is the Lord's doing, and it is marvellous in our eyes?

"Therefore say I unto you, The kingdom of God shall be taken from you, and given to a nation bringing forth the fruits thereof.

"And whosoever shall fall on this stone shall be broken: but on whomsoever it shall fall, it will grind him to powder" (Matthew 21:42-44).

This at last was sufficient for the chief priests and Pharisees to realize that Jesus was speaking about them. Angered, they sought to lay hands on him, but fearing the crowd, they decided to wait.

- ❑ Then Jesus again spoke to them with a parable, telling them of the King who bid people to a great wedding banquet. Unfortunately the invitees made light of it and disrespected the King. Not only would they not come to the banquet, they went so far as to spitefully abuse the King's servants and slew them.

> *"But when the king heard thereof, he was wroth: and he sent forth his armies, and destroyed those murderers, and burned up their city...*
>
> *"So those servants went out into the highways, and gathered together all as many as they found, both bad and good: and the wedding was furnished with guests.*
>
> *"And when the king came in to see the guests, he saw there a man which had not on a wedding garment:*
>
> *"And he saith unto him, Friend, how camest thou in hither not having a wedding garment? And he was speechless.*
>
> *"Then said the king to the servants, Bind him hand and foot, and take him away, and cast him into outer darkness; there shall be weeping and gnashing of teeth.*
>
> *"For many are called, but few are chosen."*

Jesus, then, prophesied that even though He was the Son of God, the Jews would reject and kill Him and would do likewise to His servants. Their greedy goal would be to kill the heir and seize the kingdom for themselves. *But the end result would be that the kingdom would be taken from them and given to another nation that would bear fruits.*

❑ The people of that nation who shall be heirs to the kingdom are all those who believe in Christ and belong to Him (*Galatians 3:29*).

The Apostle Peter, therefore, declared this to the saints of Jesus:

"Forasmuch as ye know that ye were not redeemed with corruptible things, as silver and gold, from your vain conversation received by tradition from your fathers; But with the precious blood of Christ, as of a lamb without blemish and without spot" (1 Peter 1:18-19).

"Ye also, as lively stones, are built up a spiritual house, an holy priesthood, to offer up spiritual sacrifices, acceptable to God by Jesus Christ.

"Wherefore also it is contained in the scripture, Behold, I lay in Sion a chief corner stone, elect, precious: and he that believeth on him shall not be confounded.

"Unto you therefore which believe he is precious: but unto them which be disobedient, the stone which the builders disallowed, the same is made the head of the corner,

"And a stone of stumbling, and a rock of offence, even to them which stumble at the word, being disobedient: whereunto also they were appointed.

"But ye are a chosen generation, a royal priesthood, an holy nation, a peculiar people; that ye should shew forth the praises of him who

hath called you out of darkness into his marvellous light:

"Which in time past were not a people, but are now the people of God: which had not obtained mercy, but now have obtained mercy" (1 Peter 2:5-10).

❑ And Paul preached to the Christians and said:

"But ye are come unto mount Sion, and unto the city of the living God, the heavenly Jerusalem, and to an innumerable company of angels, To the general assembly and church of the firstborn, which are written in heaven, and to God the Judge of all, and to the spirits of just men made perfect, And to Jesus the mediator of the new covenant, and to the blood of sprinkling, that speaketh better things than that of Abel" (Hebrews 12:22-24).

"Wherefore we receiving a kingdom which cannot be moved, let us have grace, whereby we may serve God acceptably with reverence and godly fear: For our God is a consuming fire" (Hebrews 12:28-29).

---

44 Whosoever does not confess that Jesus Christ is come in the flesh is not of God and is the spirit of antichrist:

"Hereby know ye the Spirit of God: Every spirit that

confesseth that Jesus Christ is come in the flesh is of God: And every spirit that confesseth not that Jesus Christ is come in the flesh is not of God: and this is that spirit of antichrist, whereof ye have heard that it should come; and even now already is it in the world.

"Ye are of God, little children, and have overcome them: because greater is he that is in you, than he that is in the world. They are of the world: therefore speak they of the world, and the world heareth them. We are of God: he that knoweth God heareth us; he that is not of God heareth not us. Hereby know we the spirit of truth, and the spirit of error" (1 John 4:2-6).

❑ Jews do not confess that Jesus Christ came in the flesh; therefore, they are not of God. The Jewish Talmud blasphemes Jesus, denounces him, says he was not sent by God, and was a liar who did great harm to Israel. All these are proofs that, as the Apostle John testified, the Jews possess the *"spirit of antichrist."* They are of the world and, as such, belong to Satan, who is their Father.

❑ In the second epistle of John, the Apostle speaks further on this subject, warning Christians to be wary of those who would bring a lie into the church:

"For many deceivers are entered into the world, who confess not that Jesus Christ is come in the flesh. This is a deceiver and an antichrist."

Since the Jews confess not that Jesus came in the

flesh as God and instead deny the same and go on to blaspheme Christ and attempt to deceive men by teaching them the myths and fictions in their Talmud and Kabbalah, they clearly stamp themselves as antichrists.

❏ Indeed, so wicked are the teachings of the Talmud and Kabbalah that the Jews are warned in their Talmud *(Libbre David 37)*, "To communicate anything to a Goy (gentile) about our religious relations would be equal to the killing of all the Jews, for if the Goyim knew what we teach about them, they would kill us openly."

---

45 The Scriptures say that the woman, Mystery, Babylon the Great, rides upon a beast having seven heads and ten horns. And these ten horns are kings who make war against the Lamb:

"So he carried me away in the spirit into the wilderness: and I saw a woman sit upon a scarlet coloured beast, full of names of blasphemy, having seven heads and ten horns" (Revelation 17:3).

"And there are seven kings: five are fallen, and one is, and the other is not yet come; and when he cometh, he must continue a short space" (Revelation 17:10).

❏ World Jewry has long made war against the Lamb, and in *Revelation 17:3* she (the Jews) ride upon the beast whose ten horns (kings) make war on the Lamb. The Lamb is Jesus Christ the Messiah and Saviour of humanity. Organized Jewry makes war daily against Jesus and Christianity. The ADL, AIPAC, the AJC, the Jewish Defense League, the Southern Poverty Law Center, the American Civil Liberties Union, and dozens of other groups have together filed hundreds of lawsuits seeking to prevent Christ-like behavior and to ban signs and symbols of Christ and Christianity from the workplace and from public display. Jews even make war on Christmas, campaigning to prevent store clerks from gaily saying "Merry Christmas" to customers.

Jewish organizations and groups have been able to remove the Ten Commandments from government buildings and schools, to ban prayer in schools and at public sporting events, and so on. The slightest mention of Jesus in open prayers brings the threat of lawsuits and retaliation by these satanically-inspired Jewish groups.

- ❑ Meanwhile, the Jewish producers and directors who run Hollywood and Broadway continually besiege our senses with images hostile to Christianity. They mock the Christian faith, vigorously profane the name of Jesus in their productions, and shower us with all types of immorality and debauchery.

- ❑ The Jews are responsible for new Department of Defense rules forbidding military chaplains from praying in the name of Jesus, and the display of religious scenes during Christmas holidays is expressly attacked by Jewish organizations.

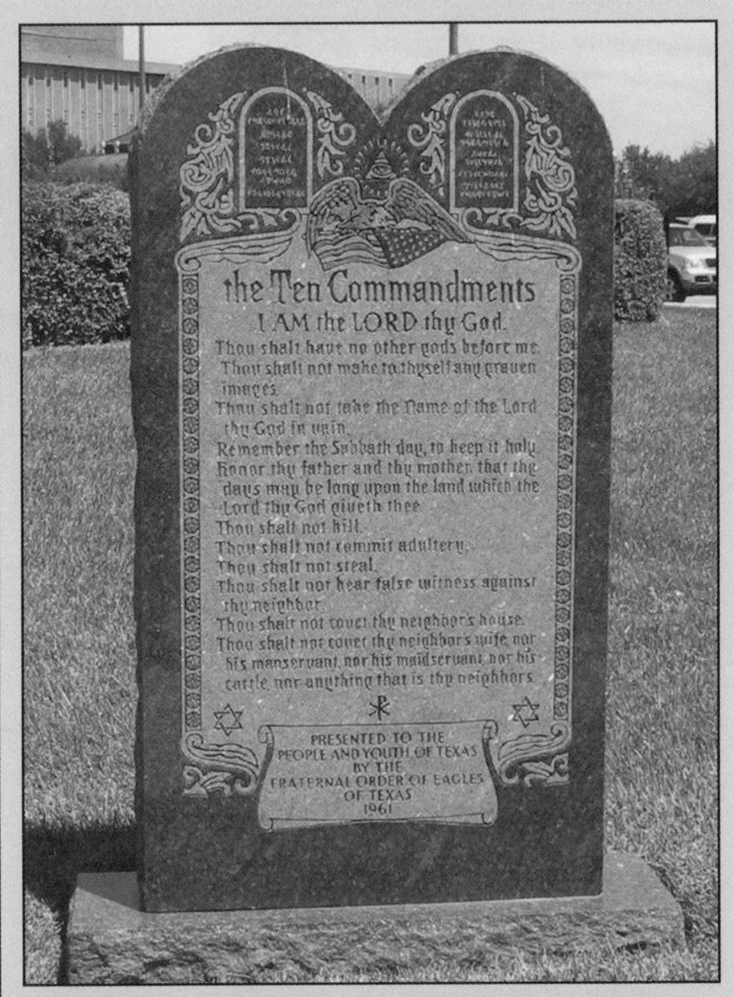

A poll taken found that less than one in five Americans agreed with a Jewish judge who ordered this Ten Commandments memorial in Texas be removed. Jewish-run organizations specialize in removing all vestiges of Christian and biblical America from public life.

- The Jew war against the Lamb even extends to the Word of God, and Jewish rabbis now demand that significant passages be stricken from the New

Testament which they deem unfavorable to Jews. Wealthy Jews have bankrolled new versions of the Holy Bible and watered down the language to make Jews look better and to uphold the unholy doctrine of Judaism and its man-made laws and commandments.

- ❑ No other religion and no other ethnic group has taken upon itself the task of eradicating Christianity and removing the very name of Jesus. Moslems actually hold Jesus up as a prophet and honor his Mother, Mary, as a virtuous woman of God. Neither Hindus nor Buddhists attack Jesus nor do they demand that his name be removed from public discourse.

These vicious attacks on the Christian faith and on the name of Jesus are exclusively of the Jews.

This great war by the Jews against the Lamb will remain until the day our Lord Jesus returns.

46

The beast will be a leader of a global empire:

"And the ten horns which thou sawest are ten kings, which have received no kingdom as yet; but receive power as kings one hour with the beast. These have one mind, and shall give their power and strength unto the beast" (Revelation 17:12-13).

"And it was given unto him to make war with the saints, and to overcome them: and power was given him over all kindreds, and tongues, and nations. And all that dwell upon the earth shall worship him,

whose names are not written in the book of life of the Lamb slain from the foundation of the world" (Revelation 13:7-8).

- ❑ World Jewry is dispersed worldwide and exercises unparalleled economic and political power in the United States and Canada, in Germany, France, Italy, and Great Britain, and even in China. As the astute Prime Minister of Malaysia, Mahatir Mohamed, stated (October 17, 2003), *"Today, the Jews rule the world by proxy. They get others to fight and die for them."*

Prime Minister Mahathir Mohamad, shown here with President George W. Bush, in 2003, at a global economic conference, stated, *"Today, the Jews rule the world by proxy. They get others to fight and die for them."*

---

47 The capital of this global empire will be Jerusalem. It is that *"great city"* referred to in the book of *Revelation.*

- ❏ That "great city" will be led by the beast and will have charge over the "kings" of the earth, who are united in a latter day ten nation federation: "And the ten horns which thou sawest are ten kings which received no kingdom as yet; but receive power as kings one hour with the beast" *(Revelation 17:12).*

  "These have one mind, and shall give their strength and power unto the beast" (Revelation 17:13).

- ❏ The "great city" is symbolically the woman, Mystery, Babylon the Great *(Revelation 17:5)*: "And the woman which thou sawest is that "great city," which reigneth over the kings of the earth" *(Revelation 17:18).*

- ❏ This "great city" of evil is ruled by the beast which rises up out of the pit *(Revelation 11:17)*. It is not only identified as the harlot, or woman, which is "Mystery, Babylon the Great," but also has a wicked and descriptive *spiritual* name: "…the great city, which spiritually is called Sodom and Egypt, where also our Lord was crucified." The latter information, "where also our Lord was crucified…" establishes the great city as none other than Jerusalem.

---

48 Many shall be beheaded for their faith in the last days:

"And I saw thrones, and they sat upon them, and judgment was given unto them: and I saw the souls

of them that were beheaded for the witness of Jesus, and for the word of God, and which had not worshipped the beast, neither his image, neither had received his mark upon their foreheads, or in their hands; and they lived and reigned with Christ a thousand years" (Revelation 20:4).

- ❑ The Talmud of the Jews contains the Noahide Laws which declare that in the future world, when Jews shall reign as divine kings over all, the penalty for Gentiles who are idolaters is *death by beheading*. The worship of Jesus is defined as idolatry in the Talmud and so all who are found "guilty" of worshipping Christ Jesus shall be killed by beheading.

- ❑ Interestingly, during the French Revolution, instigated by the Masonic Lodge and by the Order of the Illuminati—both of which were of Jewish origins—the guillotine was invented and employed. King Louis XVI and Queen Marie Antoinette lost their head to the guillotine but so did many others, royals and commoners alike.

- ❑ Today, the *Grand Orient Lodge of Freemasonry*, Paris' most influential secret society, annually celebrates a Masonic holy day in which an effigy loses its head on the guillotine. Many famous persons are members of this Lodge, including Presidents of France Sarkozy (a Jew), Francois Mitterand, and Jacques Chirac. Freemasonry is Jewish and according to former Sovereign Grand Commander Albert Pike, in *Morals and Dogma*, its rituals are based on the Kabbalah.

49 The Bible makes clear that the prideful and arrogant will not enter the Kingdom of Heaven. *I Peter 5:5-6* reminds us:

> *"Likewise, ye younger, submit yourselves unto the elder. Yea, all of you be subject one to another, and be clothed with humility: for God resisteth the proud, and giveth grace to the humble.*
>
> *"Humble yourselves therefore under the mighty hand of God, that he may exalt you in due time:"*

- ❑ The Kabbalah holds that the redeemer of Israel is the Holy Serpent, Leviathan. Leviathan is the protector and benefactor of the Jews and will rise from the abyss, lifting the Jews to reign over the earth. *Job 41:33-34* describes the fierce and mighty Leviathan beast:

  > *"Upon earth there is not his like, who is made without fear. He beholdeth all high things: he is a king over all the children of pride."*

  Leviathan is esteemed as king by the Jews. In the Kabbalah we find that he will lift them upward on the Tree of Life, toward godhood and Kether (the Crown). The Jews are, indeed, the *"children of pride."*

- ❑ The Talmud says that Jews are gods. They can therefore, sin against gentiles (the goyim) with impunity, and "If the gentile hits a Jew, the gentile must be killed" *(Talmud Sanhedrin 58 b)*.

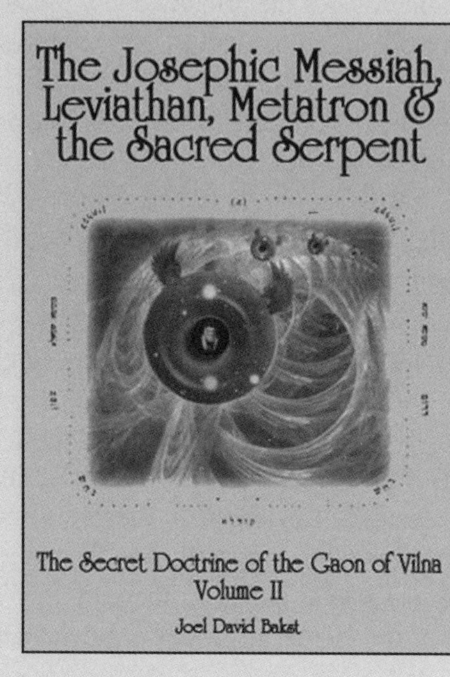

This book, by Rabbi Bakst, examines the Talmud and Kabbalah's teachings about the "Sacred Serpent." The Jews say that Leviathan is their redeemer and aide.

- ❑ The Jews say that their sages know more and are *superior* to God Himself: "A rabbi debates God and defeats Him. God admits the rabbi won the debate" *(Talmud, Baba Mezia 59 b)*.

- ❑ The writings of the rabbis are said to be superior to and more significant than the words of God: "My son, be more careful in the observance of the words of the scribes (the Talmud) than in the words of the Torah (Old Testament)" *(Talmud, Erubin 21 b)*.

50 The Bible says that, *"A doubleminded man is unstable in all his ways" (James 1:8)*. Therefore, the

antichrist will surely be doubleminded.

- ❑ The Kabbalah teaches that all things are dual in nature. Thus, male and female, black and white, and good and evil are one in unity.

- ❑ So pivotal to Judaism is this doctrine of doublemindedness considered holy and desirable that the Kabbalah teaches that the primordial Serpent, the Leviathan, said to come from the "penetrating ray of light emanating from the *Ein Sof* (or *Ain Sof*, the supreme God of the Jews)," will be redeemed and given glory and honor. "In messianic times," writes Rabbi Bakst (*The Josephic Messiah, Leviathan, Metatron, and the Sacred Serpent*, p. 100), "the Serpent will be redeemed and revealed in all of its profundity and infinite glory."

- ❑ Bakst adds: "Leviathan (the Holy Serpent) is God consciousness... Leviathan is the hidden light of existence... It is the next stage of human evolution."

  So, according to the wisdom of the Kabbalah, the Jew in the messianic era to come will be endowed with the light of Leviathan. He will be possessed of "God consciousness" and "bask in the radiance" of the Serpent of Light. "This," writes Rabbi Bakst, "is what the Torah (Old Testament), Talmud and Midrash are referring to under the umbrella of Leviathan."

  Leviathan, again, is the name of the beast that rises out of the sea *(Revelation 13:1)*. This is the beast empowered by the dragon, Satan, which "makes war with the saints of God" (Christians). This is that same beast whom God victoriously casts into the lake of fire where he will burn forever and ever.

- The Kabbalah also teaches dualism, or double-mindedness. Thus, in the kingdom age the Utopia of the Jews may be attained by *either* of two means. The Jewish individual must be supremely and utterly *evil*, or he or she might be righteous and worthy. Either path, wickedness or righteousness, involves good works.

  The famed rabbi, the Gaon of Vilna, wrote that the Jew may only ascend spiritually "through extensive and well-founded training in both extremities, i.e. from the depths of the earth (hell) to the heights of the heavens... These two extremities are interdependent... In the six hundredth year of the sixth millennium the gates of wisdom *above*, together with the well springs of wisdom *below*, will be opened up, and the world will be prepared to usher in the seventh millennium (Utopia)."

- The Kabbalah tells the Jew to *unite* both the lower and upper regions of the mind: "The upper waters represent the mystery of supernal wisdom *above*, while the lower waters represent the mystery of secular wisdom *below*. These are *united* in men's mind."

- The Leshem, another famous rabbi, explained: "In the messianic era, all spiritual impurity will be nullified, all physical substance will become transformed... By the same token all impure things will become permitted."

  "The Lord will permit what is presently forbidden." Evil will become good, and good evil. This is *doublemindedness*.

51 The prophetic word tells us that those who follow after the beast and do his evil works will refuse to repent.

> *"And the rest of the men which were not killed by these plagues yet repented not of the works of their hands, that they should not worship devils, and idols of gold, and silver, and brass, and stone, and of wood: which neither can see, nor hear, nor walk: Neither repented they of their murders, nor of their sorceries, nor of their fornication, nor of their thefts." (Revelation 9: 20-21)*

❑ The Jews gravitate toward evil and are responsible for many of earth's greatest crimes. These crimes are epitomized by their control of Hollywood and the production of worldwide pornography. The Zionist propaganda movie *The Passover Plot*, for example, cast porno star Zalman King Lefkowitz to play the part of Jesus. The blasphemous movie, *The Last Temptation of Christ*, was produced by Universal Studios, run by a Jew, Lew Wasserman. Neal Gabler's book, *An Empire of Their Own*, explains how the Jews systematically took over Hollywood and the movie industry.

❑ The TV networks are almost all owned by Jews, and Jewish comics hostile to Christianity and denigrating of Jesus are legion. Among them are HBO's Bill Maher, Roseanne Barr, and Sarah Silverman.

❑ The Jews are intent on mocking Jesus and debasing the morals of America. The monstrously perverted Jewish

Al Goldstein, editor of Jewish pornographic magazine, *Screw,* shoots the middle finger at Christianity.

pornographer Al Goldstein, the founder and editor of *Screw* magazine, bragged that the only reason Jews are involved in pornography is because they "think Christ sucks." Meanwhile, Jewish professor Nathan Abrams writes that, "Jewish involvement in porn…is the result of an atavistic hatred of Christian authority. They are trying to weaken the dominant culture of America by moral subversion."

❏ It is not only the porn industry in which the decadent Jews lead. There is also the abortion, magazine and book publishing, illegal body parts, sex trafficking, and illegal drug industries and vices. The gambling casinos of Las Vegas, New Jersey, and Macao (in China) are almost all owned by wealthy Jews. The Mafia in America was long the reserve of Jews. Meyer Lansky was head of the Mafia for many years and other, wealthy Jews continue as king pins. Wherever sin and degradation are found, Jews are close at hand.

52 Jesus declared to the Jews, *"Behold, your house is left unto you desolate" (Matthew 23:38).*

- ❑ In 70 AD, about four decades after Jesus' pronouncement, the Roman General Titus invaded Israel, tore down the Temple stone by stone, and killed thousands of Jewish inhabitants of Jerusalem. This fulfilled Christ's prophecy.

- ❑ "Desolate" means empty, of no value, abandoned. This was Jesus' prophecy. Any attempt to undo Jesus' prophecies is a sacrilege. Jesus had the Temple destroyed and Jerusalem razed. The Jewish efforts to rebuild Jerusalem and Israel, and the antichrist's rebuilding of the great Temple will bring on the Apocalypse *(II Thessalonians 2).* Israel will remain a burdensome stone until Jesus returns *(Matthew 23:39).*

53 Latter-day Israel is today populated by the fierce, warrior people known as Gog and Magog. In *Ezekiel 38*, we read this prophecy:

> *"Son of man, set thy face against Gog, the land of Magog, the chief prince of Meshech and Tubal, and prophesy against him.*
>
> *"And say, Thus saith the Lord God; Behold, I am against Thee, O Gog, the chief prince of Meshech and Tubal..."*

Who is this evil force, Gog and Magog? Why is God against Gog and Magog? We read further in *Ezekiel 38* that these people have a great army "clothed with all sorts of armor." The Scriptures say that Gog and Magog bring the warriors of many other nations with them and attack the "mountains of Israel," the people which have been "gathered from many peoples."

This invasion will occur, says the Bible, "in the latter years." Gog and Magog and all their allies "shalt ascend and come like a storm." They shall be "like a cloud to cover the land."

Over the centuries, Bible scholars have speculated about who is Gog and Magog. Some believed these people to be from Southern Russia. But most were puzzled and had no clue.

Various encyclopedias tackle this probing question, too, and some encyclopedic scholars say that the Turkic lands of Azerbaijan, Kazakhstan, Georgia, and Ukraine, south of Russia are the ancestral homes of the people who revered certain pagan deities known as Gog and Magog.

The Jewish writer Arthur Koestler, in his outstanding work, *The Thirteenth Tribe*, says that the once large and populous nation-state of Khazaria is the home of the people of Gog and Magog. But Koestler goes on to write that Khazaria, a pagan nation just south of Russia in the Caucasus, converted in the 8th through the 10th century to Judaism! The monarch of Khazaria, King Bulan, chose Judaism over its two monotheistic rivals, Christianity and Islam.

At that time, there were few Jews left in the entire world, and the peoples of Khazaria added a great number to the total population of the Jews.

Later, the nation of Khazaria was conquered by its northern neighbor, Czarist Russia. The vanquished Khazarians—mostly worshipers of Judaism by then—slowly immigrated westward to Latvia, Czechoslovakia, and especially to Poland.

It was from Poland, in 1947-48, that the Jews migrated to the new, fledgling state of Israel in the Middle East. The Jews of Israel, are, in fact, not racial Jews but, instead, are of Khazarian blood.

This fact is borne out by recent DNA scientific studies conducted by noted Jewish genetic scientists, Dr. Eran Elhaik, Dr. Ariella Oppenheim, and others. (See Texe Marrs' *DNA Science and the Jewish Bloodline*, 2013)

These scientists found that the Jews of modern-day Israel are predominantly of Turkic blood and thus have no kinship connection with the ancient Israelites. This DNA research was a shock to Israel's "Jews" who continue to dispute these well-proven scientific facts.

What we discover, then, is that the Jews of today's Israel are, in fact, ancestors of the Khazarians. And modern archaeology and other world history finds that the Khazarians were once pagans who were, traditionally, the people of Gog and Magog!

- ❑ This astonishing fact leads us, then, right to the prophecies in *Ezekiel 38*, which pictures Gog, from the land of Magog, invading the land of Israel "in the latter years."

- In 2014, the book *The Matrix of Gog*, by Daniel Patrick was published. This outstanding book confirms that almost all of today's Jews are of Khazarian, Turkic DNA. It also explains how the Jews will fulfill the Bible's prophecies regarding Gog and Magog.

- Gog and Magog are also mentioned prominently in the book of *Revelation, Chapter 2, verses 7-10*, where they play a big part in the Satanic endtime war against the saints of God.

  "And when the thousand years are expired, Satan shall be loosed out of his prison,

  "And shall go out to deceive the nations which are in the four quarters of the earth, Gog and Magog, to gather them together to battle: the number of whom is as the sand of the sea.

  "And they went up on the breadth of the earth, and compassed the camp of the saints about, and the beloved city: and fire came down from God out of heaven, and devoured them.

  "And the devil that deceived them was cast into the lake of fire and brimstone, where the beast and the false prophet are, and shall be tormented day and night for ever and ever."

- Gog and Magog, then, are Jews (converts from ancient Khazaria) who first conquer the "mountains of Israel" and then go on to "deceive the nations which are in the four quarters of the earth."

❑ Here we see prophesied a militant, reinvigorated land of Israel—today's nation of Israel, complete with nuclear bombs and other high tech armaments—amply supplied and supported by its global allies—the United States, Europe, and others—deceiving the nations throughout the earth. Through this deceit, Gog and Magog are able to gather them together to battle *"the Camp of the Saints."* This is the remnant of God, the very elect who are not deceived, the people known everywhere as Christians.

❑ This is the momentous, last days battle of planet earth, pitting the evil and mighty Gog and Magog and all their allies against the few who are in the Camp of the Saints and the beloved city. (The Saints are citizens of *heavenly*, not earthly, Jerusalem) This battle culminates in the destruction of the combined forces of evil as fire comes down from God out of heaven. Then the devil is cast into the lake of fire and brimstone (hell) where he shall be tormented for ever and ever.

Two Important Bible Prophecies— Israel's Destiny in the Last Days

54 Moses' Prophecy:

"For I know that after my death ye will utterly corrupt yourselves, and turn aside from the way which I have commanded you; and evil will befall you in the latter days; because ye will do evil in the

sight of the LORD, to provoke him to anger through the work of your hands."

---

55 Isaiah's Prophecy:

"Wherefore hear the word of the LORD, ye scornful men, that rule this people which is in Jerusalem.

"Because ye have said, We have made a covenant with death, and with hell are we at agreement; when the overflowing scourge shall pass through, it shall not come unto us: for we have made lies our refuge, and under falsehood have we hid ourselves:

"Therefore thus saith the Lord GOD, Behold, I lay in Zion for a foundation a stone, a tried stone, a precious corner stone, a sure foundation: he that believeth shall not make haste.

"Judgment also will I lay to the line, and righteousness to the plummet: and the hail shall sweep away the refuge of lies, and the waters shall overflow the hiding place.

"And your covenant with death shall be disannulled, and your agreement with hell shall not stand; when the overflowing scourge shall pass through, then ye shall be trodden down by it."

INDEX

ABOUT THE AUTHOR

Well-known author of the #1 national bestseller, *Dark Secrets of The New Age*, Texe Marrs has written books for such major publishers as Simon & Schuster, John Wiley, Prentice Hall/Arco, McGraw-Hill, and Dow Jones-Irwin. His books have sold millions of copies. He is one of the world's foremost symbologists and is a first-rate scholar of ancient history and Mystery religions.

Texe Marrs was assistant professor of aerospace studies, teaching American defense policy, strategic weapons systems, and related subjects at the University of Texas at Austin for five years. He has also taught international affairs, political science, and psychology for two other universities. A graduate *summa cum laude* from Park College, Kansas City, Missouri, he earned his Master's degree at North Carolina State University.

As a career USAF officer (now retired), he commanded communications-electronics and engineering units. He holds a number of military decorations including the Vietnam Service Medal and Presidential Unit Citation, and has served in Germany, Italy, and throughout Asia.

President of RiverCrest Publishing in Austin, Texas, Texe Marrs is a frequent guest on radio and TV talk shows throughout the U.S.A. and Canada. His monthly newsletter, *Power of Prophecy*, is distributed around the world, and he is heard globally on his popular, international shortwave and internet radio program, *Power of Prophecy*. His articles and research are published regularly on his exclusive websites: *powerofprophecy.com* and *conspiracyworld.com*.

FOR OUR NEWSLETTER

Texe Marrs offers a free sample copy of his newsletter focusing on world events, false religion, and secret societies, cults, and the occult challenge to Christianity. If you would like to receive this newsletter, please write to:

Power of Prophecy
1708 Patterson Road
Austin, Texas 78733

You may also e-mail your request to:
customerservice1@powerofprophecy.com

FOR OUR WEBSITE

Texe Marrs' newsletter is published free monthly on our website. This website has descriptions of all Texe Marrs' books, and are packed with interesting, insight-filled articles, videos, breaking news, and other information. You also have the opportunity to order an exciting array of books, tapes, and videos through our online Catalog and Sales Store. Visit our website at:

www.powerofprophecy.com

OUR SHORTWAVE RADIO PROGRAM

Texe Marrs' international radio program, *Power of Prophecy*, is broadcast weekly on shortwave radio throughout the United States and the world. *Power of Prophecy* can be heard on WWCR at 4.840 on Sunday nights at 9:00 p.m. Central Time. You may also listen to *Power of Prophecy* 24/7 on website *powerofprophecy.com.*

MORE RESOURCES FOR YOU

Books:

(For all orders, please include shipping and handling charge)

Bloody Zion—Refuting the Jewish Fables That Sustain Israel's War Against God and Man, by Edward Hendrie (544 pages) $28

Conspiracy of the Six-Pointed Star—Eye Opening Revelations and Forbidden Knowledge About Israel, the Jews, Zionism, and the Rothschilds, by Texe Marrs (432 pages) $25

Codex Magica—Secret Signs, Mysterious Symbols, and Hidden Codes of the Illuminati, by Texe Marrs (624 pages) $35

Conspiracy World—A Truthteller's Compendium of Eye-Opening Revelations and Forbidden Knowledge, by Texe Marrs (432 pages) $25

DNA Science and the Jewish Bloodline, by Texe Marrs (256 pages) $20

Holy Serpent of the Jews, by Texe Marrs (224 pages) $20

Judaism's Strange Gods, by Michael Hoffman (381 pages) $22

Matrix of Gog—From the Land of Magog Came the Khazars to Destroy and Plunder, by Daniel Patrick (160 pages) $18

On the Jews and Their Lies, by Martin Luther (240 pages) $20

Protocols of the Learned Elders of Zion (320 Pages) $20

Solving the Mystery of Babylon the Great, by Edward Hendrie (388 pages) $25

The Synagogue of Satan, by Andrew Carrington Hitchcock (320 pages) $20

Videos:

Cauldron of Abaddon—"From Jerusalem and Israel Flow a Torrent of Satanic Evil and Mischief Endangering the Whole World" (DVD) $25

Illuminati Mystery Babylon—The Hidden Elite of Israel, America, and Russia, and Their Quest for Global Dominion (DVD) $25

Marching to Zion (DVD) $20

Masonic Lodge Over Jerusalem—The Hidden Rulers of Israel, the Coming World War in the Middle East and the Rebuilding of the Temple (DVD) $25

Rothschild's Choice—Barack Obama and the Hidden Cabal Behind the Plot to Murder America (DVD) $25

Thunder Over Zion—Illuminati Bloodlines and the Secret Plan for A Jewish Utopia and a New World Messiah (DVD) $25

Please add 10% for shipping in the United States (minimum $5)
Texas residents add taxes of 6.75%
International Shipping: Please add 70% (minimum $30)

Order Now! Use your MasterCard, Visa,
Discover, or American Express
You may order from our website: www.powerofprophecy.com
Or you may phone 1-800-234-9673,
or send check or money order to:
Power of Prophecy 1708 Patterson Road, Austin, Texas 78733

Check Out This Web Site for more invaluable
books, videos, audiotapes, and for breaking news and informative
articles: www.powerofprophecy.com